To Speak the Truth

TO SPEAK THE TRUTH

*Why Washington's 'Cold War' against Cuba
Doesn't End*

FIDEL CASTRO

ERNESTO CHE GUEVARA

PATHFINDER

New York   London   Montreal   Sydney

Edited by Mary-Alice Waters

ISBN 0-87348-633-1 paper; ISBN 0-87348-634-X cloth
Library of Congress Catalog Card Number 91-75347
Manufactured in the United States of America

First edition, 1992
Fourth printing, 2000

Cover design by Eric Simpson
Cover photos: United Nations

Pathfinder
410 West Street, New York, NY 10014, U.S.A.
Fax: (212) 727-0150
E-mail: pathfinderpress@compuserve.com

PATHFINDER DISTRIBUTORS AROUND THE WORLD:
Australia (and Asia and the Pacific):
    Pathfinder, 1st floor, 176 Redfern St., Redfern, N.S.W. 2016
    Postal address: P.O. Box K879, Haymarket, N.S.W. 1240
Canada:
    Pathfinder, 851 Bloor St. West, Toronto, ON, M6G 1M3
Iceland:
    Pathfinder, Klapparstíg 26, 2d floor, 101 Reykjavík
    Postal address: P. Box 0233, IS 121 Reykjavík
New Zealand:
    Pathfinder, La Gonda Arcade, 203 Karangahape Road, Auckland
    Postal address: P.O. Box 8730, Auckland
Sweden:
    Pathfinder, Vikingagatan 10, S-113 42, Stockholm
United Kingdom (and Europe, Africa except South Africa, and Middle East):
    Pathfinder, 47 The Cut, London, SE1 8LL
United States (and Caribbean, Latin America, and South Africa):
    Pathfinder, 410 West Street, New York, NY 10014

Contents

Fidel Castro

Fidel Castro, born into a small landowning family in eastern Cuba in 1926, began his political activity while attending the University of Havana in the mid-1940s.

After Fulgencio Batista's coup d'état of March 10, 1952, Castro organized a revolutionary movement to initiate armed struggle against the U.S.-backed dictatorship. On July 26, 1953, he led an attack on the Moncada army garrison in Santiago de Cuba. Many participants were captured and murdered in cold blood; Castro and other survivors were imprisoned. Originally sentenced to fifteen years, he was released in 1955 together with his comrades as a result of an amnesty campaign. Following his release, the July 26 Movement was formed.

In July 1955 Castro left Cuba for Mexico, where he organized a guerrilla expedition to return to Cuba. On December 2, 1956, along with eighty-one other fighters, he landed in southeastern Cuba aboard the yacht *Granma*. For the next two years, Castro directed the operations of the Rebel Army and its expanding network of mass popular support from a base in the Sierra Maestra mountains. On January 1, 1959, Batista was forced to flee Cuba and shortly thereafter Rebel Army units entered Havana.

In February 1959 Castro became prime minister, a position he held until December 1976, when he became president of the Council of State and Council of Ministers. He has been commander in chief of Cuba's armed forces since 1959 and is first secretary of the Central Committee of the Communist Party of Cuba.

Ernesto Che Guevara

Ernesto "Che" Guevara was born in Argentina in 1928. After graduating from medical school in 1953, he set off to travel the Americas. While living in Guatemala in 1954, he became involved in political struggle, supporting the elected government of Jacobo Arbenz against the CIA's eventually successful attempts to overthrow it. He then escaped to Mexico, where he soon joined Fidel Castro and other Cuban revolutionaries seeking to overthrow dictator Fulgencio Batista.

In December 1956 Guevara was part of the expedition that landed in Cuba aboard the yacht *Granma* to begin the guerrilla struggle. Originally the troop doctor, Guevara became a commander of the Rebel Army.

Following Batista's fall on January 1, 1959, Guevara became one of the central leaders of the new revolutionary government. He held a number of posts, including president of the National Bank and minister of industry, and frequently represented Cuba internationally, including at the United Nations and in other world forums. As a leader of the July 26 Movement, he helped bring about the political regroupment that led to the founding of the Communist Party of Cuba in October 1965.

Guevara resigned his government posts and responsibilities in early 1965 and left Cuba to participate directly in revolutionary struggles in other countries. He initially went to the Congo and later to Bolivia, where he led a guerrilla movement against that country's military dictatorship. Wounded and captured by the Bolivian army in a CIA-organized operation on October 8, 1967, he was murdered the following day.

Introduction

For more than thirty years, Cuba has been the target of an unremitting effort by the government of the United States to rid the Americas of the revolutionary government that came to power in January 1959 with the armed popular overthrow of the Batista tyranny, a regime long nourished and protected by Washington.

In August 1991 Cuban foreign minister Ricardo Alarcón, then Havana's permanent representative to the United Nations, explained that from the beginning Washington's aggressive policy has had "the declared aim of imposing on [Cuba] the political, social and economic order which the United States authorities consider most fitting. This policy has included direct military intervention, the threat of nuclear annihilation, the instigation and carrying out of countless acts of sabotage and plans to assassinate Cuban leaders, all of which has been officially recognized by successive United States administrations and documented in detail in the United States *Congressional Record.*"

An essential element of this course, pursued for close to three and a half decades, has been an economic, commercial, and financial embargo aimed at crippling Cuba's economy. The embargo is so sweeping that it includes a total prohibition on Cuba's acquisition of foodstuffs, medicine, and medical supplies and equipment of United States origin. Currency restrictions prevent U.S. residents wishing to see Cuba for themselves from exercising their basic constitutional right to freedom of travel.

Despite strong protests by some of Washington's closest allies such as Canada, Britain, and France, the U.S. government has also tried, through various forms of coercion and economic blackmail, to impose its embargo laws beyond U.S. borders. Through legal entanglements and measures such as preventing ships engaged in trade with Cuba from docking in transit at U.S. ports, Washington attempts—albeit with diminishing success—to prevent its competitors from trading in the Cuban markets that U.S. businesses have abandoned.

The obvious question is *why*. Why this thirty-plus-year history of implacable hostility that has no parallel in modern times? Even the blockade of revolutionary and Napoleonic France following the 1789 overthrow of the old feudal order—a blockade imposed by the reactionary powers of the Continent led by the British crown—was of shorter duration than the twentieth-century U.S. embargo of Washington's small island neighbor.

Why does the U.S. government persist? The reasons are nowhere explained more clearly than in the four speeches that follow in the pages of this book.

These speeches were delivered over a twenty-year period before bodies of the United Nations by the two most authoritative international representatives, and individual products, of the Cuban revolution, Fidel Castro and Ernesto Che Guevara. The issues they address—and the answers they give—are as timely today as they were when Castro and Guevara originally disrupted the diplomatic decorum of those halls by speaking the truth.

All these speeches were printed in Cuban publications at the time they were given; new English translations have been made for this volume by Michael Taber and Michael Baumann.

In September 1960, in the address that opens this collection, Cuban prime minister Fidel Castro refers in passing to John F. Kennedy, then the Democratic Party candidate for president of the United States, as an "illiterate and ignorant millionaire" who doesn't understand that "it is not possible to carry out a revolution over the opposition of the peasants." He then quickly adds, to general laughter, that such opinions about Kennedy do not imply any preference for his opponent Richard Nixon, then the vice president of the United States.

Interrupted by the president of the General Assembly and asked to consider whether it is "right and proper" to express such views at the rostrum of the United Nations, Castro promises his full cooperation in abiding by the conventions of UN debate.

"I have no intention of offending anyone," Castro insists. "It is somewhat a question of style and, above all, a question of confidence in the assembly."

As such exchanges confirm, the appearances of Guevara and Castro before the United Nations are marked above all by the absence of empty diplomatic formulae, boring and ritualistic statements for the record, or mock-serious bombast. From the rostrum of the United Nations they speak not to the rich, powerful, and cynical of the world, but for and to the immense majority of toiling humanity, defending the "righteous rebellion of the peoples" who have been "denied the right to life and to human dignity."

At the center of all four speeches is the character, history, and centrality of United States commerce and foreign policy in relationship to Cuba, to Latin America, and to the rest of the semicolonial world exploited for so long by the imperialist world order. The reader is struck by the fact that the "new" world order proclaimed by Washington following the collapse of the old Stalinist regimes of Eastern Europe and the Soviet Union has brought no relief from the economic and social realities documented by Castro and Guevara. The instability, inequities, and explosive social conflicts of the disintegrating old world order have only sharpened.

* * *

Castro's trip to the United States in September 1960 to address the United Nations General Assembly coincided with a decisive turning point in the revolution. In response to Washington's accelerating political, economic, and military aggression, which Castro concretely documents in his speech, virtually all imperialist-owned banks and industries in Cuba, along with the largest holdings of Cuba's capitalist owners, were nationalized between August and October 1960. Day after day, tens of thousands of Cuban working people occupied fields and factories and mobilized in the streets to guarantee that everything from AT&T, to Standard Oil, to United Fruit, to Bacardi Rum and the Havana Hilton—all the most hated symbols of U.S.-organized and -supported exploitation and degradation—became the property of the Cuban people. The transition to a planned socialist economy had begun.

Castro's defense of the revolution before the General Assembly captures the power—and tension—of this historic moment, as Cuba's working people took their own future in hand, knowing full-well the confrontation that lay ahead.

As the Cuban leader explains to the world through his address before the General Assembly, the conflicts with Washington began in the first months of the revolution over payments and indemnities to the U.S.-owned telephone and electrical monopolies and for land holdings affected by the first agrarian reform law adopted in May 1959.

Notes from the U.S. State Department began to rain down on Cuba. They never asked us about our problems, not even to express sympathy or because of their responsibility in creating the problems. They never asked us how many died of starvation in our country, how many were suffering from tuberculosis, how many were unemployed. No. Did they ever express solidarity regarding our needs? Never. Every conversation we had with the representatives of the U.S. government centered around the telephone company, the electricity company, the problem of the land owned by U.S. companies. The question they asked was how we were going to pay. Naturally, the first thing they should have asked was not "How?" but "With what?"

This was a poor, underdeveloped country with 600,000 unemployed, with an extremely high rate of disease and illiteracy, whose reserves had been sapped, that had contributed to the economy of a powerful country to the tune of $1 billion in ten years. Where were we to find the means to pay for the land affected by the agrarian reform, at the prices they wanted?

What were the wishes raised by the U.S. State Department concerning U.S. interests being affected? They demanded three things: "speedy, efficient, and just payment." Do you understand that language? "Speedy, efficient, and just payment." That means, "Pay this instant, in dollars, and whatever we ask." [*Applause*]

We were not 150 percent communists at that time, [*Laughter*] we just appeared slightly pink. We were not confiscating land. We simply proposed to pay for it in twenty years, and in the only way we could—by bonds that would mature in twenty years, at 4.5 percent interest amortized annually.

The choice before the revolutionary government, Castro notes, was either to betray the interests of the Cuban people by abandoning the land reform, or risk aggression by the powerful northern neighbor. "As far as the president of the United States [Dwight D. Eisenhower] is concerned, of course, what we have done is a betrayal of our people," Castro says. But "he surely would not have considered it a betrayal if, instead of being true to its people, the revolutionary government had rather been true to the monopolies that were exploiting Cuba."

Cubans were warned that the agrarian reform had ruined the country, Castro points out. "It's possible [Washington] imagined that without the all-powerful monopolies we Cubans were incapable of producing sugar." But clearly, "if the revolution had ruined the country, the United States would have had no need to attack us," he notes. "They would have left us alone and the U.S. government would have appeared as a very noble and honorable government while we ruined the nation, proving that you cannot make a revolution because revolutions ruin countries."

History, and the course pursued by the U.S. government, proved the opposite, however. "Cuba had not been ruined and it therefore had to be ruined," Castro explains.

That was the origin of the course that Washington has pursued for more than thirty years.

In his 1964 address to the United Nations-sponsored conference on Trade and Development in Geneva, Switzerland, Ernesto Che Guevara quotes then U.S. secretary of state Dean Rusk as saying there could be no improvement in relations with Cuba so long as it represented a threat to the Americas. "That threat can be ended to Washington's satisfaction only with the overthrow of the Castro regime by the Cuban people," Rusk had said. "We regard that regime as temporary."

The Cuban revolution has proven far less temporary than Rusk and his successors ever dreamed. As Castro and Guevara document throughout these pages, Washington's implacable hatred of it is rooted in the example set by the Cuban people in daring to defy the prerogatives of capital and instead lead laboring millions to carry out a genuine social revolution and selflessly aid those under attack—from Vietnam to Panama, from southern Africa to Nicaragua. The Cuban people have successfully stood up to unrelenting U.S. aggression in all its varied forms.

For that reason the working people of Cuba continue to be punished; and in defense of that revolution they continue to defy, and withstand, Washington's pressures today.

* * *

Guevara's 1964 address to the Geneva trade conference details in clear and scientific terms the meaning for the great majority of humanity of the international economic institutions established at the end of World War II under the guiding hand of the all-powerful imperialist victor, the United States. Guevara's explanation of the workings of the International Monetary Fund, the General Agreement on Tariffs and Trade (GATT), the International Bank for Reconstruction and Development (the World Bank), the Inter-American Development Bank, and other such entities reads like a primer for understanding the interimperialist trade wars, the monetary and banking crises, and the political antagonisms sharpening today.

Guevara presents the inevitable economic and social consequences for countries dominated by imperialism and predicts the crushing impact of the approaching foreign debt crisis facing the underdeveloped countries. Guevara needed no crystal ball, however. He simply describes how finance capital works. The debt crisis would not be an aberration, a momentary pathological condition, disfiguring an otherwise "healthy" and beneficial relationship between the major capitalist powers and the semicolonial world, he explains. Finance capital cannot act otherwise.

Using Cuba as an example, Guevara documents the fundamentals of imperialist exploitation, explaining why "the penetration of capital from the developed countries is the essential condition" for economic dependence. He points to the subtle and not-so-subtle forms of economic aggression: "Loans granted on onerous terms; investments that place a given country under the power of the investors; almost total technological subordination of the dependent country to the developed country; control of a country's foreign trade by the big international monopolies; and in extreme cases, the use of force as an economic power."

Guevara dissects the results of the Alliance for Progress proclaimed by President Kennedy in 1961 in response to the dangerous example set by the Cuban revolution. Offering it as a case study in the devastating results of imperialist "aid,"

Guevara notes that during the three months of the Geneva trade conference alone, Latin American countries would lose directly or indirectly almost $1.6 billion in the forms of interest payments on foreign investments and loans, capital flight, and loss of purchasing power through deterioration in terms of trade. The $2 billion a year in loans Washington was to deliver through the imperialist banks as part of the Alliance for Progress would only accelerate this transfer to imperialist coffers of wealth created by the toilers of Latin America.

"Latin America's experience with the real results of this type of 'aid' . . . has been a sad one," Guevara says. "For this very reason it may serve as a lesson for other regions and for the underdeveloped world in general."

Fifteen years later, in the October 1979 speech that is the final selection in this book, Fidel Castro returns to the fraud of loan packages cloaked as "development aid." In his address to the United Nations General Assembly on behalf of the Movement of Nonaligned Countries, televised throughout North America and around the world, Castro points to the rapidly accelerating indebtedness of the developing countries even then, several years before the devastating explosion of the debt crisis in the early 1980s. "Most of the funds received from abroad by the developing nations are earmarked to cover their trade balances and negative current accounts, to renew their debts, and to make interest payments," Castro says. This revolving fund to enrich the imperialist banks did not result in increased production and distribution of food for the great majority, or sustainable indigenous industrial development, let alone permanently improved health care, schools, or housing.

Per capita food production in Africa in 1977 was 11 percent below that of ten years earlier, Castro notes. This was only one measure of the widening gulf between the conditions of life for the toiling masses of the underdeveloped world and the wealth accumulated by the handful of families on top of the imperialist pyramid.

In July 1991, at the first Ibero-American Summit meeting held in Guadalajara, Mexico, Castro updated the Latin American realities explained by Guevara almost thirty years earlier.

> For the tenth consecutive year, the economic crisis continues to affect all our economies. The per capita Gross National Product today does not exceed the level reached 13 years ago. The import-export price ratio is 21 percent worse than at the beginning of the 1980s. The foreign debt remains above $400 billion, despite the fact that the region has transferred resources abroad to the tune of $224 billion in just eight years. Inflation reached unprecedented levels during this period.
>
> The policies decided upon by the big economic powers and the international financial institutions under their control have not led to development but have made 250 million people poorer; they have failed to bring in [net] foreign capital but have facilitated the flow of capital toward the developed countries. . . .
>
> If the total value of the net foreign exchange leaving Latin America each year were converted to gold, it would be greater than all the gold and silver that Spain and Portugal took away during 300 years.

At the 1964 World Conference on Trade and Development in Geneva, Guevara explains that all the phrases and formulae about "equal treatment and reciprocal concessions between developed and underdeveloped countries" amount to one thing: perpetuating the interests of the former, thus guaranteeing that the real gap between these countries will widen. That's what "freedom of competition" means under capitalism, Guevara said.

To imperialism, free trade does not mean "the right of all nations to unrestricted freedom of trade . . . the right of all countries to freely arrange the shipment of their goods by sea or air and to move them freely throughout the world without hindrance," Guevara explains. To the contrary, both free trade and protectionism are policy tools of competing imperialist interests.

Genuinely fair trade, not free trade, can be the only foundation for world peace or economic development. "And fairness, in this context, is not equality; fairness is the inequality needed to enable the exploited peoples to attain an acceptable standard of living."

Throughout these pages both Guevara and Castro affirm and explain that a new world economic order based on such objectives can be achieved only if the oppressed and exploited of the world take the road of anticapitalist revolution. Imperialism is the cause of the evils from which the majority of the world's people suffer, Guevara tells the Geneva conference. "The only way to solve the problems now besetting humanity is to eliminate completely the exploitation of dependent countries by developed capitalist countries," Guevara says, "with all the consequences that implies."

The more than thirty-year-long U.S. embargo against Cuba testifies eloquently that the Yankee colossus is convinced that this objective—the complete elimination of imperialist exploitation and oppression, "with all the consequences that implies"—remains Cuba's international goal and inspires its revolutionary course.

*   *   *

Cuba's support for the national liberation struggles of the peoples of Africa is one of the threads that runs through this collection of speeches.

Guevara was on his way to Africa in December 1964 when he addressed the United Nations General Assembly. He spent three months in Africa meeting with leaders of many national liberation movements and newly independent African countries. Shortly after returning to Cuba in early 1965, he formally resigned his government posts as well as party and military responsibilities and went back to Africa to fight alongside the guerrilla forces in the Congo attempting to break the imperialists' stranglehold on the vast, mineral-rich country today known as Zaire.

Speaking before the General Assembly, Guevara denounces the role of United Nations troops in the Congo, "under whose auspices" the assassins of Congolese independence leader Patrice Lumumba had "acted with impunity." He condemns the massacres being perpetrated there by "Western civilization" and the "imperial white man" in the name of humanitarianism. And he makes clear his future course. "All free men of the world must be prepared to avenge the crime of the Congo," he tells the delegates to the United Nations.

"Those peoples whose skins are darkened by a different sun, colored by different pigments, constitute the majority" in the General Assembly, Guevara says. "And they fully and clearly understand that the difference between men does not lie in the color of their skin, but in the forms of ownership of the means of production, in the relations of production."

More than a quarter century later, at a rally of tens of thousands in Matanzas, Cuba, on July 26, 1991, African National Congress president Nelson Mandela paid tribute to the Cuban revolution's aid to African independence struggles. He acknowledged the impact of the contributions made by "the great Che Guevara," whose revolutionary actions in Africa in the mid-1960s, Mandela said, "were too powerful for any prison censors to hide from us."

"What other country can point to a record of greater selflessness than Cuba has displayed in its relations with Africa?" Mandela asked. He pointed especially to the fifteen-year effort of several hundred thousand Cuban volunteers to aid the Angolan government in defeating the South African apartheid army's invasion of that country.

It was in prison when I first heard of the massive assistance that the Cuban internationalist forces provided to the people of Angola, on such a scale that one hesitated to believe, when the Angolans came under combined attack of South African, CIA-financed FNLA, mercenary, UNITA, and Zairean troops in 1975.[1]

We in Africa are used to being victims of countries wanting to carve up our territory or subvert our sovereignty. It is unparalleled in African history to have another people rise to the defense of one of us. . . .

Your presence and the reinforcement of your forces in the battle of Cuito Cuanavale was of truly historic significance.[2] The crushing defeat of the racist army at Cuito Cuanavale was a victory for the whole of Africa . . . a turning point in the struggle to free the continent and our country from the scourge of apartheid!

Mandela also took note of the aid the African National Congress had received from Cuba when vicious repression by the apartheid regime in the 1960s left the ANC "no choice but to do what every self-respecting people, including the Cubans, have done—that is, to take up arms to win our country back from the racists."

When the ANC needed weapons and training, Mandela said, "we approached numerous Western governments for assistance and we were never able to see any but the most junior ministers. When we visited Cuba we were received by the highest officials and were immediately offered whatever we wanted and needed. That was our earliest experience with Cuban internationalism."

* * *

The lesson of the Congo experience that Guevara points to in the General Assembly speech was clear. It was paid for by the life of Patrice Lumumba, the Congo's first president, and by untold thousands of others who mistakenly believed that military forces operating under the United Nations flag came as "peacekeepers." Only too late did they learn that blue helmets and blue flags were there to defend imperialist interests, as Guevara describes.

But the lesson of the Congo, like the earlier lesson of the Korean War—also fought under the banner of the United Nations—was not lost on the leaders of the Cuban revolution. The Cuban government has always categorically rejected, as a violation of Cuban sovereignty and independence, any and all demands for United Nations "inspection" or "supervision" of anything in Cuba.

As the Congo example confirms, the United Nations never uses economic or military force harmful to imperialist interests. Like the International Monetary Fund, World Bank, and other institutions born of U.S. paternity at the end of World War II, the United Nations was structured from the beginning to assure and facilitate the perpetuation of the capitalist world order. The fifteen-member Security Council, the body in which the UN's executive powers are vested, operates on the basis of the veto privilege, with each of the Council's five permanent members—the governments of Britain, China, France, Russia (formerly the Soviet Union), and the United States—enjoying the right to veto any proposal that comes before that body. Nonpermanent members have no veto power.

Speaking to the General Assembly in 1960, Fidel Castro notes with alarm U.S. president Eisenhower's proposal that United Nations "observers" and emergency "forces" be ready "to promote peaceful change as well as to assist economic and social progress" in the "developing areas." "We wish to state here," Castro says, "that the Cuban delegation does not agree with such an emergency force until all peoples of the world can feel sure that these forces will not be put at the disposal of colonialism and imperialism. [*Applause*] This is especially so inasmuch as our countries can at any moment become the victim of the use of such forces against the rights of our peoples."

In the wake of one of the most brutal imperialist assaults on an underdeveloped country in history—the 1990–91 U.S.-led

war on Iraq, organized under the flag of the United Nations—
Castro's warning of thirty years earlier has a prophetic ring. It
required no genius or supernatural powers, however, just a scientific understanding of the nature of imperialism and the courage to speak the truth.

"Since the United Nations was born," Cuban ambassador
Alarcón told the Security Council on August 9, 1990, "we have
seen how certain great powers have sought to use the Council
as a tool for their own strategic interests rather than as a body
working for the maintenance of international peace and security." That understanding, as shown in the pages that follow,
has shaped Cuba's defense of the interests of the oppressed in
the world forum of the United Nations.

❋   ❋   ❋

High on the list of the Cuban government's permanent priorities has been defense of the rights of peoples most directly
oppressed by the imperialist power the Cuban people know best.
The Cuban delegation's demonstrative decision in 1960 to accept the invitation extended to them by Malcolm X, on behalf
of the Harlem Welcoming Committee, to stay at Harlem's Hotel Theresa is recounted in the appendix to this book. In December 1964, while Guevara was in New York to address the
UN General Assembly, he accepted an invitation from Malcolm
X to speak at a rally of the Organization of Afro-American
Unity held at the Audubon Ballroom in Harlem. At the last
minute, security considerations prevented Guevara from appearing. But he sent a message that Malcolm himself, calling
the Cuban revolutionary leader "a very good friend of ours,"
insisted on reading to the audience. Guevara sent "the warm
salutations of the Cuban people and especially Fidel, who
remembers enthusiastically his visit to Harlem a few years
ago."

"The United States intervenes in Latin America invoking
the defense of free institutions," Guevara tells the General As-

sembly. That 1964 visit occurred barely four months after Harlem had exploded in what was the first of the major rebellions that occurred in the Black ghettos of the United States in the 1960s. (It was also barely four months after the U.S. Congress passed the infamous Tonkin Gulf resolution, authorizing the massive escalation of the U.S. war against Vietnam; Guevara condemns this rapidly expanding aggression against the peoples of Indochina in his remarks.) "The time will come," Guevara says,

> when this assembly will acquire greater maturity and demand of the United States government guarantees for the lives of the Blacks and Latin Americans who live in that country, most of them U.S. citizens by origin or adoption.
>
> Those who kill their own children and discriminate daily against them because of the color of their skin; those who let the murderers of Blacks remain free, protecting them, and furthermore punishing the Black population because they demand their legitimate rights as free men—how can those who do this consider themselves guardians of freedom?

Puerto Rico's right to independence and national sovereignty is also a cause the Cuban people defend with an internationalist conviction buoyed by the closely shared history of the two nations. Guevara's tribute to Puerto Rican patriot Pedro Albizu Campos in his 1964 address to the General Assembly spotlights the brutal treatment meted out to Puerto Rican nationalists in the federal prisons of the United States—a country that, contrary to its fondest self-image, remains a colonial power even as the twentieth century comes to a close.

In 1979 Castro once again used his New York visit in a demonstrative way, organizing time to meet with Rafael Cancel Miranda, Lolita Lebrón, and Irving Flores. The three historic champions of Puerto Rico's independence struggle had been released from U.S. prisons the previous month after serving twenty-five-year sentences for a 1954 armed demonstration, in the visitors' gallery of the House of Representatives, against Washington's colonial policies.

* * *

When Fidel Castro returned to the United Nations General Assembly in 1979, it was not to speak as Cuba's head of state and government. Instead, Castro speaks on behalf of the ninety-five members of the Movement of Nonaligned Countries, "representing the immense majority of humanity . . . joined together in our determination to change the present system of international relations, based as it is on injustice, inequality, and oppression."

Cuba was a founding member of the Movement of Nonaligned Countries, constituted in Belgrade in 1961, and has played an active role in shaping its course. "The quintessence of the policy of nonalignment," Castro affirms here on behalf of the Movement, "involves the struggle against imperialism, colonialism, neocolonialism, apartheid, racism including Zionism, and all forms of foreign aggression, occupation, domination, interference, or hegemony, as well as against great-power and bloc policies."

The principles of peaceful coexistence defended by the Nonaligned Movement as the basis for international relations, Castro says, include the unconditional "right of peoples under foreign and colonial domination to self-determination. They include independence; sovereignty; the territorial integrity of states; the right of every country to put an end to foreign occupation and to the acquisition of territory by force; and the right to choose its own social, political, and economic system."

Bound together by a common history of colonialism and imperialist domination, the Nonaligned Movement is economically and politically heterogeneous. Member countries range from those whose governments are closely aligned with imperialist powers; to countries such as the former

Yugoslavia under the Tito leadership, which was trying to gain some leverage vis-à-vis the Soviet Union; to Cuba, with its proletarian internationalist foreign policy. Nonaligned summit meetings are diplomatic battlegrounds among these contending forces, with the leaders of the host country able to exert considerable influence in shaping the agenda and casting the resolutions adopted.

In 1979, despite concerted efforts by the U.S. government, the Nonaligned summit meeting was held in Havana, and the rotating chairmanship devolved upon Fidel Castro, president of the host country. The Havana summit came a matter of weeks after the victorious revolutionary overthrow of the U.S.-backed dictatorship of Anastasio Somoza in Nicaragua. That same year the Pol Pot regime in Cambodia had fallen, under the combined blows of an internal revolt and the intervention of the Vietnamese army; the shah of Iran had been toppled by a mass revolutionary uprising; and Grenadian dictator Eric Gairy had been overthrown by a popular revolutionary movement under the leadership of Maurice Bishop.

These historic events are the backdrop to Castro's address "on behalf of the children of the world who do not even have a piece of bread."

Carefully delineating the deteriorating economic conditions faced by the toiling masses of the underdeveloped world, Castro outlines the minimum conditions that must be met by the developed capitalist countries to effect any change.

Unequal exchange is ruining our peoples. It must end!

Inflation, which is being exported to us, is crushing our peoples. It must end!

Protectionism is impoverishing our peoples. It must end!

The existing imbalance in the exploitation of the resources of the sea is abusive. It must be abolished!

The financial resources received by the developing countries are insufficient. They must be increased!

Arms expenditures are irrational. They must cease and the

funds thus released must be used to finance development!

The international monetary system prevailing today is bankrupt. It must be replaced!

The debts of the least-developed countries, and of those in a disadvantageous position, are burdens impossible to bear, to which no solution can be found. They must be cancelled!

Indebtedness oppresses the rest of the developing countries economically. There must be relief!

The economic chasm between the developed countries and the countries seeking development is not narrowing but widening. It must be closed!

If these demands of the underdeveloped countries are incompatible with the continued existence of the current world economic order, Castro makes clear, then capitalism must go. "Why should some people go barefoot," he asks, "so that others may travel in expensive cars? Why should some live only thirty-five years, so that others may live seventy? Why should some be miserably poor, so that others may be exaggeratedly rich? . . . Why then civilization?"

"In any case," Castro tells the millions in North America and around the world watching his televised address, "the prospect of a world without capitalism is not too frightening to us revolutionaries."

In closing his remarks Castro offers a glimpse of the world panorama now unfolding in the 1990s, as the shadow of economic depression spreads, social tensions sharpen, and the opening guns of World War III are heard from Iraq to the Balkans. "I have not come here as a prophet of revolution," Castro states. "I have not come here to ask or to wish that the world be violently convulsed. I have come to speak of peace and cooperation among the peoples. And I have come to warn that if we do not peacefully and wisely resolve the present injustices and inequalities, the future will be apocalyptic."

Reading this volume today helps us to better understand

and act in the increasingly apocalyptic world in which we live. It also explains why Washington's unending "cold war" and inhuman economic embargo against Cuba go on—a backhanded tribute to the fact that the Cuban revolution lives.

Mary-Alice Waters

SEPTEMBER 1992

The case of Cuba is the case of all underdeveloped countries

Fidel Castro

From the moment Fidel Castro arrived in New York City on September 18, 1960, until his departure ten days later, the Cuban leader was at the center of an intense political battle. Never before or since has so much attention been focused on an appearance at the United Nations.

Castro was one of a number of heads of state scheduled to address the opening of the Fifteenth Session of the UN General Assembly. Others included Nikita Khrushchev of the Soviet Union, Gamal Abdel Nasser of Egypt, Jawaharlal Nehru of India, Kwame Nkrumah of Ghana, Harold MacMillan of Britain, Josip Broz Tito of Yugoslavia, U.S. president Dwight Eisenhower, and others. Yet it was the Cuban prime minister who was in the spotlight.

Throughout his stay, Castro was the target of a systematic campaign of harassment by U.S. authorities. The State Department ordered him confined to the island of Manhattan. A U.S. court ordered the seizure of the Cubana Airlines plane that brought him to New York, pending settlement of a claim by a U.S. company against the Cuban government.

A campaign of slander and vilification was waged in the media. Articles in major dailies contained reports of Cubans plucking chickens in their hotel rooms and holding lavish parties with alleged prostitutes. Abandoning all pretense of objective journalism, newspapers portrayed Castro as a "bearded fanatic" who "frothed at the mouth" and "ranted and raved."

One of the biggest sources of controversy concerned the Cubans' housing accommodations. Prior to Castro's arrival, numerous hotels had refused to provide rooms to the Cubans. Eventually the Shelburne Hotel in midtown Manhattan agreed to take them in. The day after Castro arrived, however, the hotel management demanded $10,000 in cash as a deposit against possible damages. Terming this an act of extortion, the Cuban delegation packed their bags and moved to the Hotel Theresa in Harlem.

This act of solidarity with African-Americans and the battle against racial discrimination in the United States, unprecedented for a visiting head of state, made headlines around the world. Among those who facilitated the move was Malcolm X, at the time a minister of the Nation of Islam. An account of the meeting at the Hotel Theresa between Castro and Malcolm X is printed at the back of the book as an appendix.

As word spread that the Cuban delegation was on its way, two thousand Harlem residents gathered in the rain outside the Hotel Theresa, chanting "We want Castro!" For days thereafter, crowds of up to ten thousand came out to show their solidarity and to catch a glimpse of the Cuban leader. Atop the Hotel Theresa the Cuban flag was raised.

The highlight of the political battle waged by the Cuban delegation to counter Washington's attempts to isolate them came on the afternoon of Monday, September 26, 1960, when Castro mounted the rostrum at the United Nations General Assembly hall to deliver the following address.

UNITED NATIONS

Fidel Castro

The case of Cuba is the case of all underdeveloped countries

Address to General Assembly
September 26, 1960

Mr. President;
Distinguished representatives:

Although I am said to speak at great length, you may rest assured that I shall strive to be brief and to present here what we believe needs to be presented. I shall also speak slowly to assist the interpreters.

Some may think we are very annoyed and upset by the treatment received by the Cuban delegation. That is not the case. We understand perfectly well why these things have happened, and we are therefore not upset. You may rest assured that Cuba will make every effort to bring about understanding in the world. But of this you may be certain: we shall speak frankly.

It is extremely expensive to send a delegation to the United Nations. We of the underdeveloped countries do not have many resources to squander, and when we do spend money in this fashion it is because we wish to speak frankly in this meeting of representatives of practically all the countries of the world.

The speakers who preceded me have expressed their concern about problems of interest to the entire world. We too are concerned with these problems. However, in the case of Cuba a special circumstance exists: Cuba should itself be a world concern. Different speakers who have spoken here have said, quite correctly, that among the problems now facing the world is that of Cuba. In addition, Cuba itself has problems of concern to us and to our people.

Much has been said of the universal desire for peace. This is the desire of all peoples and, as such, it is the desire of our people too. But this peace that the world wishes to preserve is something we Cubans have not been able to enjoy for some time. The dangers that other peoples of the world may consider more or less distant are problems that for us are very immediate. It has not been easy to come here to this assembly to speak of the problems of Cuba; it has not been easy for us to come here.

I do not know whether we should consider ourselves privileged. Do we, the members of the Cuban delegation, represent the worst type of government in the world? Do we, the members of the Cuban delegation, merit the mistreatment we have received? Why has our delegation been singled out? Cuba has sent many delegations to the United Nations in the past; Cuba has been represented in the United Nations by many different persons. Yet it was we who were singled out for such exceptional measures: confinement to the island of Manhattan; notice to all hotels not to rent us rooms; hostility; and—under the pretext of security—isolation.

All of you, distinguished delegates, represent your respective countries and not yourselves as individuals. For that reason, the matters affecting each of you as individuals should be of concern because of what you represent. Perhaps not one of you, upon your arrival in New York City, has had to suffer the personal mistreatment, the physically humiliating treatment, that was meted out to the president of the Cuban delegation.

I am not trying to stir up anyone here in this assembly. I am merely stating the truth. The time has come for us to take the floor and speak. Much has been said about us. For many days the newspapers have been talking about us, and we have held our peace, since we cannot defend ourselves against attacks in this country. But the time to speak the truth has now come, and we will not hesitate to do so.

As I have said, we had to put up with degrading and humiliating treatment, efforts at extortion, and eviction from our hotel. We then went to another hotel, doing everything in our power to avoid difficulties. We refrained from leaving our hotel rooms, going nowhere except to this assembly hall of the United Nations on the few occasions we have come here, in addition to accepting an invitation to a reception at the Soviet mission. Yet even this was not enough for us to be left in peace.

There has been considerable Cuban emigration to the United States. More than 100,000 Cubans have come to this country during the past twenty years, forced by economic reasons to leave their homeland, the land in which they would have preferred to live, and the land to which they would like to return. These Cubans here devoted themselves to work and they respected the laws. And naturally, they felt close to their country and to the revolution. They never had problems.

But one day a different type of visitor began to arrive in the United States. War criminals began to arrive. Individuals began to arrive who in some cases had murdered hundreds of our compatriots.[3] It did not take long for the publicity they were getting here to give them encouragement. It did not take long for the authorities to give them encouragement. And naturally that encouragement has been reflected in their behavior; it is the cause of the frequent incidents between these individuals and the Cuban people who many years earlier had come to this country and have been working here in an honest way.

One of these incidents, provoked by those who draw encouragement from the systematic campaigns against Cuba and the connivance of the authorities, caused the death of a young girl.[4] This was a tragic event for which we all feel sorrow. The guilty ones were not the Cubans living here, much less we, the members of the Cuban delegation. Yet undoubtedly you have all seen the headlines in the newspapers stating that "pro-Castro groups" had killed a ten-year-old girl.

And with the hypocrisy characteristic of those responsible for relations between Cuba and the United States, a White House spokesman immediately issued a statement to the world practically accusing the Cuban delegation of the crime. And of course, His Excellency, the distinguished representative of the United States of America to this assembly did not miss the opportunity of adding his voice to the farce, sending a telegram to the Venezuelan government and a telegram of condolence to the family—as if they felt compelled to give an explanation in the United Nations for something the Cuban delegation was virtually held responsible for.

But it did not stop there. After we were forced to leave one of the hotels of this city and were coming to the United Nations headquarters, and while other efforts were being made, a modest hotel of the Black people of Harlem took us in.

The reply by this hotel came while we were speaking with the secretary-general. Nevertheless, an official of the State Department did everything in his power to prevent us from taking up residence there. Suddenly, as if by magic, hotels began springing up all over New York. Hotels that had previously refused us rooms now offered them to us for free. But we, out of elementary gratitude, accepted the hotel in Harlem. We felt we had earned the right to be left in peace. But no, they did not leave us in peace.

As soon as we arrived in Harlem, since nobody could stop us from staying there, the campaign of slander and defamation began. News began to be spread that the Cuban delegation had taken up lodging in a brothel.[5] For some, a modest hotel in Harlem, a hotel inhabited by the Black people of the United States, must obviously be a brothel. They have also heaped slander on the Cuban delegation, not even respecting its female members.

Were we the type of men they desperately seek to depict us

as, then imperialism would not have lost hope—as it did long ago—of buying us off or seducing us in some way. Imperialism long ago lost its hope of getting us back, a hope that was groundless from the start. Rather than stating that the Cuban delegation took up rooms in a brothel, they should admit that imperialist finance capital is a prostitute that cannot seduce us—and not necessarily the "respectful prostitute" of Jean-Paul Sartre.[6]

Let us speak of the problem of Cuba. Some of you may be well informed, others not—it all depends on the sources of information. As far as the world is concerned, the problem of Cuba that has arisen in the last two years is a new one. Previously, there were few reasons for the world to know that Cuba existed. For many it was something like an appendage of the United States. Even for many U.S. citizens, Cuba was seen as a colony of the United States. As far as the map was concerned, that was not so; Cuba was colored differently from the United States. But in reality that was the case.

How did our country become a colony of the United States? It was not by origin; the individuals who colonized the United States were not the same ones who colonized Cuba. The ethnic and cultural roots of Cuba are very different, and these roots grew stronger over centuries.

Cuba was the last country of the Americas to free itself from Spanish colonial rule, to cast off the Spanish colonial yoke—no offense meant to His Excellency, the representative of the Spanish government. And because it was the last, Cuba had to struggle the hardest. Spain had one last foothold in the Americas and defended it tooth and nail. Our people, small in numbers, scarcely a million inhabitants at that time, had to stand alone for nearly thirty years confronting an army that was considered one of the strongest in Europe.[7] Against the small population of Cuba the Spanish government mobilized as many troops as it had used to fight against the independence struggles of all the South American countries combined. Half a million Spanish soldiers fought against the heroic and indomitable desire of our people to be free. For thirty years Cubans fought alone for their independence; thirty years that also helped lay the foundation for our country's love of freedom and independence.

But according to the opinion of John Quincy Adams, a United States president at the beginning of the last century, Cuba was a fruit, an apple on the Spanish tree ready to fall, as soon as it ripened, into the hands of the United States.[8]

The Spanish power had exhausted itself in Cuba. Spain no longer had either the men or the economic resources to continue the fight in Cuba. Spain was defeated. The apple had apparently ripened, and the U.S. government held out its hands. It was not merely one apple that fell; a number of apples fell into its open hands. Puerto Rico fell—the heroic Puerto Rico that had begun its struggle for independence at the same time as Cuba. The Philippine Islands fell, as did several other Spanish possessions.

But the means used to dominate our country had to be different. Our country had waged a tremendous struggle and world opinion was on its side. So the means had to be different.

The Cubans who had fought for our independence, who at that very moment were giving their blood and their lives, sincerely believed in the joint resolution of the U.S. Congress of April 20, 1898, which declared that "Cuba is, and by right ought to be, free and independent." The people of the United States sympathized with the Cuban struggle. This joint declaration adopted by the U.S. Congress was the law by which war was declared on Spain.[9]

But that illusion was ended by a cruel deception. After two years of military occupation of our country, the unexpected happened. At the very moment when, through a Constituent Assembly, the people of Cuba were drafting the constitution of the republic, a new law was passed by the U.S. Congress, a law proposed by Senator Platt, of such unhappy memory for Cuba. That law stated that Cuba's constitution must contain a stipulation granting the U.S. government the right to intervene in Cuba's political affairs, and to lease certain parts of Cuba for naval bases or coaling stations. In other words, according to a law passed by the legislative body of a foreign country, Cuba's constitution had to contain a stipulation with those provisions. The drafters of our constitution were clearly told that without the amendment the occupation forces would not be withdrawn. That is to say, the legislative body of a foreign country imposed upon our country, by force, its right to intervene and its right to lease bases or naval stations.[10]

It would be a good thing for countries just entering the United Nations, countries just beginning their independent life, to bear our history in mind. They may find similarities awaiting them along their own road, and if not they, then those who may come after them, or their children or grandchildren—although it seems to us we shall not have to wait that long.

At this point a new colonization of our country began. This included the acquisition of the best agricultural land by U.S. firms, concessions of Cuban natural resources and mines, concessions of public services for purposes of exploitation, commercial concessions, concessions of all types. All these things, together with the constitutional right to intervene in our country, transformed our country from a Spanish colony into a U.S. colony.

Colonies do not speak. Colonies are not heard from until they are granted permission to express themselves. That is why our colony and its problems were unknown to the rest of the world. In geography books there appeared yet another flag, yet another coat of arms, there was yet another color on the map. But there was no independent republic. No one should be deceived; by deceiving ourselves all we do is look ridiculous. Let no one be deceived: there was no independent republic. There was a colony where orders were given by the ambassador of the United States.

We are not ashamed of having to proclaim this. On the contrary, we are proud that we can now say: Today no embassy rules our people; our people themselves are the rulers! [*Applause*]

Once again, the Cuban nation had to resort to arms to achieve independence, and this was finally attained after seven bloody years of tyranny. Tyranny by whom? Tyranny by the forces in our country who were nothing but the instruments of those who dominated our country economically.[11]

How can an unpopular system inimical to the interests of the people stay in power other than by force? Do we have to explain to the representatives of our sister republics of Latin America what military tyrannies are? Do we have to explain to them how they have kept themselves in power? Do we have to explain to them the classic history of many of those tyrannies? Do we have to explain to them what kept them in power? Do we have to explain to them what national and international interests kept them in power?

The military group that tyrannized our country was based on the most reactionary sectors of the nation and, above all, on the foreign interests that dominated our country's economy. Everybody here knows—and we believe that even the U.S. government recognizes it—that this was the type of government preferred by the monopolies. Why? Because with force you can repress every demand by the people. With force you can repress strikes for better living conditions. With force you can repress movements by peasants to own the land. With force you can repress the most deeply felt aspirations of the nation.

That is why governments based on force were the ones preferred by the makers of U.S. policy. That is why governments based on force were able to stay in power for so long. And that is why governments based on force still rule in Latin America.

Naturally, whether one receives or does not receive the support of the U.S. government depends on circumstances. For example, the U.S. government now says it opposes one of these governments based on force, that of Trujillo. But it does not say it is against other governments based on force—those of Nicaragua or Paraguay, for example. In Nicaragua there is no longer a government based on force; it is a monarchy almost as constitutional as that of England, where the reins are handed down from father to son.[12]

The same would have occurred in our own country. Fulgencio Batista's government based on force was the type most suited to the U.S. monopolies in Cuba, but it was obviously not the type most suited to the Cuban people. Therefore, the Cuban people, at a great cost in lives, threw that government out.

When the revolution came to power, what did it find? What "marvels" did the revolution find when it came to power in Cuba? First of all, the revolution found that 600,000 Cubans, able and ready to work, were unemployed—as many, proportionally, as were jobless in the United States during the Great Depression that shook this country, and which almost produced a catastrophe here. This is what we confronted in my country—permanent unemployment. Three million out of a population of a little more than six million had no electricity, possessing none of its advantages and comforts. Three and a half million out of a total population of a little more than six million lived in huts, in shacks, and in slums, without the most minimal sanitary facilities. In the cities, rents took almost one-third of family income. Electricity rates and rents were among the highest in the world.

Some 37.5 percent of our population were illiterate; 70 percent of the rural children lacked teachers; 2 percent of our population suffered from tuberculosis—that is to say, 100,000 persons out of a little more than six million. Ninety-five percent of the children in rural areas suffered from parasites. Infant mortality was astronomical. Life expectancy was very low. On the other hand, 85 percent of the small farmers were paying rent on their land of up to 30 percent of their gross income, while 1.5 percent of the land-owners controlled 46 percent of the total area of the country. Of course, the proportion of hospital beds to the number of inhabitants was ridiculously low compared with countries that have even halfway decent medical services.

Public services, the electricity and telephone companies, all belonged to U.S. monopolies. A major portion of banking, importing, and oil refining; the majority of sugar production; the best land; and the most important industries in all fields in Cuba belonged to U.S. companies.

The balance of payments in the last ten years, from 1950 to 1960, has been favorable to the United States vis-à-vis Cuba to the extent of $1 billion. This is without taking into account the hundreds of millions of dollars extracted from the public treasury by the corrupt officials of the dictatorship and later deposited in U.S. or European banks. One billion dollars in ten years! This poor and underdeveloped Caribbean country with 600,000 unemployed was contributing to the economic development of the most economically developed country in the world!

This was the situation that confronted us. Yet it should not surprise many of the countries represented in this assembly. For what we have said about Cuba is but an X-ray view that could be applied to many of the countries represented here.

What alternative was there for the revolutionary government? To betray the people? As far as the president of the United States is concerned, of course, what we have done is a betrayal of our people. And he surely would not have considered it a betrayal if, rather than being true to its people, the revolutionary government had instead been true to the monopolies that were exploiting Cuba.

At the very least, please take note of the "marvels" confronting the revolution when it came to power. They were no more and no less than the usual marvels of imperialism, which are themselves no more and no less than the marvels of the "free world" as far as the colonized countries are concerned.

We cannot be blamed for 600,000 unemployed, 37.5 percent illiteracy, 2 percent with tuberculosis, and 95 percent with parasites. Not at all! Until that moment none of us figured in our country's destiny. Until that moment what determined the country's destiny was the monopolies, and the rulers who served the interests of the monopolies. Did anyone object? No, no one objected. Did this bother anyone? No, this did not bother anyone. The monopolies went about their business, and these were the results.

What was the state of the nation's reserves? When the tyrant Batista came to power there was $500 million in the treasury. It was a decent amount had it been invested in the country's economic development. But when the revolution came to power, only $70 million remained in the treasury.

Did they ever show any concern for the economic development of the country? No, never! That is why we were so amazed, and are still amazed, when we hear it said here how very much concerned the U.S. government is for the fate of the countries of Latin America, Africa, and Asia. And it continues to amaze us, because we had the results of fifty years.

What has the revolutionary government done? What is the crime committed by the revolutionary government to warrant the treatment we have been given here? Why do we have such powerful enemies?

Did the problems with the U.S. government arise at the very beginning? No, they did not. Was our desire when we came to power to seek out international problems? No, it was not. No revolutionary government coming to power wants international problems. What it wants is to devote itself to solving its own problems. What it wants, like any government truly concerned with its country's progress, is to carry out such a program.

The first unfriendly act perpetrated by the government of the United States was to throw open its doors to a gang of murderers and bloodthirsty criminals. These were men who had murdered hundreds of defenseless peasants, who for many, many years had never tired of torturing prisoners, of killing right and left. These criminals were received by this country with open arms. We were deeply amazed. Why this unfriendly act toward Cuba by the U.S. authorities? Why this act of hostility? At the time we did not quite understand. Now we clearly see the reasons.

Was that policy in keeping with a correct treatment of Cuba, with correct relations between the United States and Cuba? No, and the injured party was Cuba. We were the injured party, because the Batista regime had been kept in power with the aid of the government of the United States. The Batista regime had been kept in power with the aid of tanks, planes, and weapons supplied by the government of the United States. The Batista regime had been kept in power thanks to the use of an army whose officers were instructed and trained by a military mission of the government of the United States. And we hope that no official of the United States will dare to deny this.

When the Rebel Army arrived in Havana at the most important military base of that city, it met the U.S. military mission. The army of Batista was one that had collapsed; it was an army that had been beaten and had surrendered. We could easily have considered these foreign officers who had trained the enemies of the people to be prisoners of war. Yet this was not our approach. We merely asked the members of that military mission to go home. We did not need their lessons; after all, their pupils had been beaten.

I have here a document. Do not be surprised at its appearance. This torn document is an old military pact, by virtue of which the Batista dictatorship had received generous assistance from the U.S. government. It is rather interesting to note what it says in Article 2:

> The government of the Republic of Cuba commits itself to make efficient use of the assistance it receives from the government of the United States of America in conformity and pursuant to the present agreement, in order to carry out the plans of defense accepted by both governments, pursuant to which the two governments would take part in important missions for the defense of the Western Hemisphere, and unless previous agreement is obtained from the government of the United States . . .

—I repeat:

> . . . and unless previous agreement is obtained from the government of the United States of America such assistance will

not be devoted to other ends than those for which such assistance has been given.

That assistance was used to fight the Cuban revolutionaries, and for that purpose it obviously had received the consent of the U.S. government. Even when an embargo on sending arms to Batista was solemnly declared a few months before the end of the war—after over six years of military assistance—the Rebel Army nevertheless had documentary proof that the dictatorship's forces had been supplied with three hundred rockets, to be fired by air.[13]

When Cubans living in this country submitted these documents to U.S. public opinion, the U.S. government could find no other explanation than to say we were mistaken. They said the United States had not supplied new weapons to Batista's army, that they had merely exchanged some rockets of a different calibre that were the wrong size for the dictatorship's planes, supplying them instead with new rockets that did fit its planes—and that were in fact fired at us when we were in the mountains.

This was certainly a novel way of explaining an unexplainable contradiction. According to this, it was not assistance. Perhaps it was a form of "technical aid."

Why did all this make our people angry? After all, everyone here, even the most naive, knows that in these modern times, given the revolution that has taken place in military technology, the weapons from the last war have become obsolete for modern warfare. Fifty tanks or armored cars and a few obsolete aircraft cannot defend a continent or a hemisphere. They are useful, however, for oppressing unarmed peoples, for intimidating peoples. They are useful for defending the monopolies. That is why these hemispheric defense pacts might better be described as "pacts to defend U.S. monopolies."

The revolutionary government began to take its first steps. The first was a 50 percent reduction in rents paid by families. This was a very just measure since, as I said earlier, there were families paying up to one-third of their income for rent. The people had been the victims of housing speculation; urban real estate had also been subject to speculation, to the detriment of the entire Cuban people. But when the revolutionary government reduced rents by 50 percent, there were those who were considerably upset; yes, a few who owned the buildings and apartment houses were upset. But the people rushed into the streets rejoicing, as they would in any country—even here in New York—if rents were reduced by 50 percent for all families. But it caused no problems with the monopolies. Some of the U.S. companies owned large buildings, but they were relatively few in number.

Then another law was passed, a law cancelling the concessions that had been granted by the Batista dictatorship to the telephone company, which was a U.S. monopoly. Aided by having a population without means to defend itself, valuable concessions had been obtained. The revolutionary government cancelled those concessions and reestablished the prices for telephone services that had existed previously. This was the first conflict with the U.S. monopolies.

The third measure was the reduction of electricity rates, which had been among the highest in the world. This led to the second conflict with the U.S. monopolies. Already they were beginning to paint us as Reds, simply because we had clashed with the interests of the U.S. monopolies.

Then came another law, an essential law, an inevitable law—inevitable for the Cuban people and inevitable, sooner or later, for all the peoples of the world, at least those who have not done so. This was the Agrarian Reform Law.[14] Naturally, everybody agrees with agrarian reform in theory. Nobody would dare to deny it; nobody except an ignoramus would dare to deny that agrarian reform in the underdeveloped countries of the world is one of the essential conditions for economic development. In Cuba, even the owners of the vast estates agreed with agrarian reform—only they wanted an agrarian reform that suited them, like the type defended by many theorists.

Above all, they wanted the type of agrarian reform that is not carried out, as long as it can be avoided. Agrarian reform is something that is recognized by the economic bodies of the United Nations. It is something over which nobody argues. In our country it was indispensable. More than 200,000 peasant families lived in the countryside without land with which to plant essential foodstuffs. Without agrarian reform our country could not have taken the first step toward development. And we took that step. We instituted an agrarian reform. Was it radical? Yes, it was a radical agrarian reform. Was it very radical? No, it was not a very radical agrarian reform. We carried out an agrarian reform adjusted to the needs of our development, to the possibilities of agricultural development. In other words, we carried out an agrarian reform that would solve the problem of peasants without land, that would solve the problem of essential foodstuffs, that would solve the great unemployment problem on the land, and that would end the frightful poverty that existed in the rural areas of our country.

That was when the first major difficulty arose. In the neighboring Republic of Guatemala the same thing happened. When the agrarian reform came about in Guatemala, problems arose.[15] And I notify my colleagues of Latin America, Africa, and Asia with complete honesty that when they plan a just and fair agrarian reform they must be ready to confront situations similar to the one we faced, especially if the best land and the largest holdings are in the hands of the U.S. monopolies, as was the case in Cuba. [*Ovation*]

It's possible we may later be accused of giving bad advice in this assembly, which is not our intention. [*Applause*] It is not our intention to keep anybody awake at night. We are expressing facts—although facts are enough to keep many people awake at night.

Then the question of payments and indemnities came up. Notes from the U.S. State Department began to rain down on Cuba. They never asked us about our problems, not even to express sympathy or because of their responsibility in creating the problems. They never asked us how many died of starvation in our country, how many were suffering from tuberculosis, how many were unemployed. No. Did they ever express solidarity regarding our needs? Never. Every conversation we had with the representatives of the U.S. government centered around the telephone company, the electricity company, and the problem of the land owned by U.S. companies. The question they asked was how we were going to pay. Naturally, the first thing they should have asked was not "How?" but "With what?"

This was a poor, underdeveloped country with 600,000 unemployed, with an extremely high rate of disease and illiteracy, whose reserves had been sapped, that had contributed to the economy of a powerful country to the tune of $1 billion in ten years. Where were we to find the means to pay for the land affected by the agrarian reform, at the prices they wanted?

What were the wishes raised by the U.S. State Department concerning U.S. interests being affected? They demanded three things: "prompt, adequate, and effective compensation." Do you understand that language? "Prompt, adequate, and effective compensation." That means, "Pay this instant, in dollars, and whatever we ask." [*Applause*]

We were not 150 percent communists at that time, [*Laughter*] we just appeared slightly pink. We were not confiscating land. We simply proposed to pay for it in twenty years, and in the only way we could—by bonds that would mature in twenty years, at 4.5 percent interest amortized annually. How could we have paid for this land in dollars? How could we have paid on the spot, and how could we have paid whatever they asked? It was ludicrous.

It is obvious that under those circumstances, we had to choose between either carrying through an agrarian reform or not doing so. If we chose not doing so then our country's dreadful economic situation would continue indefinitely. And if we did carry out the agrarian reform, then we faced incurring the enmity of the government of the powerful neighbor to the north.

We chose to carry out the agrarian reform.

Clearly someone from the Netherlands or any other country in Europe would be quite surprised by the size of the limits we set to landholdings because they were so big. The maximum amount of land set forth in the Agrarian Reform Law was 400 hectares [1,000 acres]. In Europe 400 hectares is a true estate. In Cuba, there were U.S. monopolies that had up to 200,000 hectares—I repeat, 200,000 hectares, in case anyone thinks he has misheard. Under these circumstances, an agrarian reform reducing the maximum limit to 400 hectares was, for these monopolies, an inadmissible law.

But in our country the land was not the only thing in the hands of the U.S. monopolies. The principal mines were also in the hands of the monopolies. For example, Cuba produces large amounts of nickel, and all the nickel was controlled by U.S. interests. Under the Batista dictatorship, a U.S. company called Moa Bay had obtained such a juicy concession that in a mere five years—mark my words, in a mere five years—it sought to amortize an investment of $120 million. A $120 million investment amortized in five years!

Who had given the Moa Bay company this concession through the intercession of the U.S. ambassador? Quite simply, the dictatorship of Fulgencio Batista, the government that was there to defend the interests of the monopolies. And what is more—and this is an indisputable fact—it was completely tax-free. What were these enterprises going to leave for the Cubans? The empty, used-up mines, the impoverished land—all without having contributed in the slightest to the economic development of our country.

So the revolutionary government passed a mining law that obliged these monopolies to pay a 25 percent tax on the export of minerals.

The attitude of the revolutionary government had already been too bold. It had clashed with the interests of the international electricity trust; it had clashed with the interests of the international telephone trust; it had clashed with the interests of the international mining trusts; it had clashed with the interests of the United Fruit Company; it had clashed, in short, with the most powerful interests of the United States, which, as you know, are closely linked with one another. This was more than the U.S. government—that is, the representatives of the U.S. monopolies—could tolerate.

Then a new stage of harassing our revolution began. I will pose a question to anyone who objectively analyzes the facts, who is ready to think honestly and not parrot the UPI and the AP, who is ready to think with their own head and draw their own conclusions, who is ready to look at things without prejudice, sincerely, and honestly: Are the things done by the revolutionary government grounds to decree the destruction of the Cuban revolution? No, they are not.

But the interests that were adversely affected by the Cuban revolution were not concerned about Cuba; they were not being ruined by the measures of the Cuban revolutionary government. That was not the problem. The problem was that these same interests own the wealth and natural resources of the majority of the peoples of the world.

So the Cuban revolution had to be punished for its stance. Punitive actions of every type—including the destruction of those insolent Cubans—had to be carried out against the revolutionary government.

On our honor we swear that up to that time we had not had the opportunity to even exchange letters with the distinguished prime minister of the Soviet Union, Nikita Khrushchev. That is to say that, when the U.S. press and the international news agencies that supply information to the world were saying that Cuba was a Red government, a "Red menace" ninety miles from the United States, with a government dominated by communists, the revolutionary government had not even had the opportunity of establishing diplomatic or commercial relations with the Soviet Union.

But hysteria can go to any length; hysteria is capable of making the most unlikely and absurd claims. But of course, let no one for a moment think we are going to make a "mea culpa" here. There will be no mea culpa. We do not have to apologize to anyone. What we have done we have done with our eyes wide open and, above all, fully convinced of our right to do it! [*Prolonged applause*]

Then the threats began against our sugar quota.[16] The cheap philosophy of imperialism began to demonstrate its nobility, its selfish and exploitative nobility. It began to demonstrate its kindness to Cuba, declaring that they were paying us a preferential price for sugar, amounting to subsidizing Cuban sugar— a sugar that was not so sweet for Cubans since we were not the owners of the best sugar-producing land or of the largest sugar mills. Furthermore, that claim hid the true history of Cuban sugar, of the sacrifices that had been imposed on Cuba, of the many times Cuba had been economically harmed.

Earlier it was not a question of quotas; it was a question of customs tariffs. By virtue of one of those agreements made "between the shark and the sardine,"[17] the United States, through an agreement they called a "reciprocal agreement," obtained a series of concessions for its products. This enabled them to compete easily and displace from the Cuban market the products of its "friends" the British and the French—as often happens among "friends." In exchange for this, certain tariff concessions were granted for our sugar which, on the other hand, could be unilaterally changed by the will of Congress or the U.S. government. And that is what happened. When they deemed it in their interests they raised the tariff, and our sugar could not enter. Or if it did, it did so facing a disadvantage in the U.S. market.

As World War II approached, the tariffs were reduced. Since Cuba was obviously the supplier of sugar closest to home, that source of sugar had to be assured. So the tariffs were lowered and production was encouraged. During the war years, when the price of sugar was up in the stratosphere throughout the world, we were selling our sugar to the United States at a low price, despite the fact that we were its only supplier. When the war ended our economy collapsed.

The errors committed in selling that raw material were paid for by us. At the end of the First World War, for example, prices went up enormously. There was tremendous encouragement to production. Then a sudden fall of prices occurred that ruined Cuba's sugar mills, which conveniently fell into the hands of— I'll let you guess—U.S. banks, because when the Cuban nationals went bankrupt, the U.S. banks in Cuba became wealthy. This was the situation that continued up through the 1930s.

The U.S. government set up a system of quotas, trying to find a formula that would reconcile its need for supplies with the interests of its domestic producers. The quotas were to be based upon the historical share of the market of the various suppliers, and Cuba's historical share would have been almost 50 percent of the U.S. market. However, when the quota was set up, our share was reduced to 28 percent, and the few advantages granted us by that law were gradually taken away in subsequent laws. Naturally the colony depended on the colonial power. The economy of the colony had been organized by the colonial power. The colony had to be subordinated to the colonial power. And if the colony took measures to declare itself free from the colonial power, the colonial power would take measures to crush her.

So, conscious of our economy's dependence on the U.S. market, the U.S. government began to issue a series of warnings that our quota would be reduced.

Concurrently, other activities were taking place in the United States: the activities of the counterrevolutionaries.

One afternoon an airplane coming from the north flew over one of our sugar mills and dropped a bomb. This was a strange and unheard-of event, but we knew full well where that plane came from. On another afternoon another plane flew over our sugarcane fields and dropped a few incendiary bombs. These events, which began sporadically, continued systematically.[18]

One afternoon, while a number of U.S. tourist agents were visiting Cuba as part of an effort by the revolutionary government to promote tourism as a source of the nation's income, a U.S.-built plane—one of those used in the Second World War—flew over Havana, dropping pamphlets and a few hand grenades. Naturally some antiaircraft guns went into action. The result was more than forty victims, between the grenades dropped by the plane and the antiaircraft fire since, as you know, some of the shells explode on contact. As I said, the result was more than forty victims. These included children with their entrails torn out, and old men and old women.[19] This was not the first time. No, young girls and boys, the elderly, men and women, were often killed in the villages of Cuba by U.S. bombs supplied to the dictator Batista.

On another occasion, eighty workers were killed in a mysterious explosion—too mysterious—aboard a ship bringing Belgian weapons into our country. This occurred following great efforts by the U.S. government to prevent the Belgian government from selling us weapons.[20]

There have been dozens of victims in the war: eighty families were left orphaned by that explosion; forty victims of an airplane calmly flying over our territory. The U.S. authorities denied that these planes took off from U.S. territory. But the plane was sitting right there in its hangar. One of our magazines published a photograph of this plane in its hangar, and then the U.S. authorities seized the plane. Then, of course, an account of the affair was issued to the effect that this was not very important and that the victims had not died from the bombs but from the antiaircraft fire. Meanwhile those responsible for this crime were wandering about peacefully in the United States, where they were not even prevented from continuing their acts of aggression.

I take this opportunity to tell His Excellency, the representative of the United States, that there are many mothers in Cuba who are still waiting to receive a telegram of condolence for the children murdered by U.S. bombs.

The planes came and went. There was no proof—although you must define what you mean by proof. The plane was right there, photographed and seized. Yet we were told this plane had not dropped any bombs; it is not known how the U.S. authorities were so well informed. Pirate aircraft continued to fly over our territory dropping incendiary bombs. Millions upon millions of pesos were lost in the burning of sugarcane fields. Many working people who saw this wealth destroyed, a wealth that was now theirs, were themselves burned or wounded in the struggle against the persistent and tenacious bombings by these pirate aircraft.

Then one day, while flying over one of our sugar mills, a plane blew up when its bomb exploded, and the revolutionary government had the opportunity of gathering the remains of the pilot. It was in fact a U.S. pilot, whose papers were found, and it was a U.S. plane and we found all the proofs about the airfield from which he had taken off. That plane had passed over two bases in the United States.[21]

Now it was a case that could not be denied; it was clear the plane had come from the United States. This time, in view of the irrefutable proof, the U.S. government did give an explanation to the Cuban government. Its conduct in this case was not the same as in the U-2 case.[22] When it was proved that the planes were coming from the United States, the U.S. government did not proclaim its right to burn our cane fields. On this occasion, the U.S. government apologized, and said it was sorry. Well, we were lucky, after all, because after the U-2 incident the U.S. government did not even apologize; it proclaimed its right to fly over Soviet territory. Too bad for the Soviets! [*Applause*]

But we do not have many antiaircraft batteries and the planes continued to come until the sugar harvest was over. When there was no more sugarcane, the bombings stopped. We were the only country in the world to suffer this harassment, although I do recall that at the time of his visit to Cuba President Sukarno [of Indonesia] told us that we were not the only ones, that they too had problems with U.S. planes flying over their territory. I don't know if I've committed an indiscretion here; I don't expect so. [*Laughter and applause*]

The fact of the matter is that at least in this peaceful hemisphere, we were the one country that, without being at war with anyone, had to stand the constant attack of pirate planes. How could those planes come and go from U.S. territory with impunity? We invite the delegates here to ponder this, and we also invite the people of the United States—if by chance they have the opportunity of knowing the facts being discussed here—to ponder this matter. Because according to the statements of the U.S. government itself, U.S. territory is completely protected against any air incursion, and U.S. air defenses are infallible. It is said that the air defenses of the world they call "free"—because, so far as we are concerned, we became free on January 1, 1959—are impregnable. If this is the case, how is it that planes—and I'm not talking about supersonic planes, but simple propeller planes flying barely 150 miles an hour—how is it that these planes are able to come and go from U.S. territory at will? How can they go through two bases and come back over these two same bases without the U.S. government even being aware that these planes are coming and going from their territory?

It means one of two things. Either the U.S. government is lying to the U.S. people and the United States is defenseless against aerial incursions, or the U.S. government was an accomplice in these aerial incursions. [*Applause*]

The aerial incursions finally ended, and then came economic aggression. What was one of the arguments presented by the enemies of the agrarian reform? They said that the agrarian reform would cause chaos in agricultural production; that production would diminish considerably and that the U.S. government was concerned that Cuba might not be able to fulfill its commitments to the U.S. market.

That was the first argument, and I think that at least the new delegations here in the General Assembly should familiarize themselves with some of these arguments, because they may one day have to answer similar arguments that agrarian reform will ruin their country.

That was not the case. Had the agrarian reform ruined the country, had agricultural production decreased, then the U.S. government would not have had to carry out its economic aggression.

Did they sincerely believe what they said when they asserted that the agrarian reform would bring about a decrease in production? Perhaps they believed it. Every person believes what he makes himself believe. It's possible they imagined that without the all-powerful monopolies we Cubans were incapable of producing sugar. Perhaps they even believed we were ruining the country. Clearly if the revolution had ruined the country, the United States would have had no need to attack us. They would have left us alone and the U.S. government would have appeared as a very noble and honorable government while we ruined the nation, proving that you cannot make a revolution because revolutions ruin countries.

But that is not the case. There is living proof that revolutions do not ruin countries, and it has been supplied by the U.S. government. It has proved many things, but among them it has proved that revolutions do not ruin countries while imperialist governments do try to ruin countries.

Cuba had not been ruined and it therefore had to be ruined. Cuba needed new markets for its products, and we could honestly ask all the delegates present if there is any country that does not want to sell what it produces. Is there any country that does not want to increase its exports? We wanted our exports to increase, and this is what all countries want, it's a universal law. Only selfish interests could oppose the universal interest in commercial exchange, which is one of the oldest aspirations and needs of humanity.

We wanted to sell our products and we went in search of new markets. We signed a trade agreement with the Soviet Union, according to which we would sell one million tons of sugar in return for a certain number of Soviet products or articles.[23] Surely no one can say this is improper. There may be some who do not make such agreements because certain interests object. We did not have to ask permission of the State Department to sign a trade agreement with the Soviet Union, because we considered ourselves and will always consider ourselves a truly independent and free country.

As more of our sugar began to be sold, we received the big blow. By request of the executive branch of the U.S. government, Congress approved an act under which the president of the United States was empowered to reduce the import of sugar from Cuba to whatever limits he deemed appropriate.[24] The economic weapon was used against our revolution. The justification for this stance had already been prepared by the mass media. A campaign had been carried out for a long time, because in the United States you know full well that the monopolies and the mass media are completely intertwined.

The economic weapon was used. At one fell swoop our sugar quota was cut by almost a million tons—sugar that had already been produced for distribution in the U.S. market. The goal was to deprive our country of the resources needed for development, to reduce our country to impotence in order to attain political objectives.

Such a measure had been expressly prohibited by regional international law. As all the Latin American representatives here know, economic aggression is expressly condemned by regional international law. Nevertheless, the government of the United States violated that law, using the economic weapon and cutting our sugar quota by almost a million tons—and that was that; they could do it.

What could Cuba do when confronted by that reality? Turn to the United Nations. Go to the UN to denounce the political and economic aggression, to denounce the incursions by pirate aircraft, to denounce the economic aggression—in addition to the constant interference by the U.S. government in our country's political affairs and its subversive campaigns against the revolutionary government of Cuba.

So we turn to the United Nations. The UN has powers to investigate these matters. The UN, in the hierarchy of international organizations, stands at the head. It has authority even above that of the Organization of American States. We also wanted to bring the problem to the UN because we understand full well Latin America's economic dependence on the United States.

The United Nations is informed of the matter. It asks the Organization of American States to investigate. The OAS meets. Very good. And what was to be expected? That the OAS would protect the aggrieved country? That the OAS would condemn the political aggression against Cuba? And above all that the OAS would condemn the economic aggression against our country? This might have been expected; after all, we were a small nation, a member of the Latin American community.

Besides, we were not the first victimized country, neither the first nor the last. Mexico had already been militarily attacked more than once. A large part of Mexico's territory was seized in a war. On that occasion the heroic sons of Mexico, draping themselves in the Mexican flag, threw themselves from the castle of Chapultepec rather than surrender. Those were the heroic sons of Mexico![25] [*Applause*]

And that was not the only aggression. That was not the only time that U.S. troops trampled on Mexican territory. Nicaragua was invaded, and for seven years there was the heroic resistance of Augusto César Sandino. Cuba was attacked more than once; and so was Haiti and the Dominican Republic.[26]

Guatemala was also attacked. Who here can honestly deny the involvement of the United Fruit Company and the U.S. State Department in the overthrow of the legitimate government of Guatemala? I understand that some consider it their official duty to be discreet on this matter, and may even be capable of coming up here and denying it. But in their conscience they know we speak the simple truth.

Cuba was not the first victim of aggression. Cuba was not the first country threatened by aggression. In this hemisphere everybody knows that the U.S. government has always imposed its law, the law of the mightiest. And in accordance with this law it has suppressed the Puerto Rican nationality and has maintained its control over that island. In accordance with that law it seized the Panama Canal and continues to hold the Panama Canal. So this was nothing new.

Our country should have been defended by the OAS, but it was not defended. Why not? Here we must go to the heart of the matter and not merely to the surface. If we stick to the letter of the law, then we have guarantees. If we stick to reality, however, we have no guarantee whatsoever because reality imposes itself over and above the law set forth in international codes. And this reality is that a small country attacked by a powerful government was not defended and could not be defended.

But what happened [at the OAS meeting] in Costa Rica?[27] Lo and behold, by an ingenious miracle there was no condemnation of the United States or the U.S. government in Costa Rica! (I wish to avoid here any misunderstanding that we are confusing the government of the United States with the people of the United States.) The U.S. government was not condemned in Costa Rica for the sixty incursions by pirate aircraft. The U.S. government was not condemned for the economic and other aggressions. No, the Soviet Union was condemned! How extraordinary! We had not been attacked by the Soviet Union. No Soviet aircraft had flown over our territory. Yet in Costa Rica they condemned the Soviet Union for interference.

The Soviet Union had only said that in the event of military aggression against our country, they could, figuratively speaking, support the victim with Soviet missiles. Since when is support for a small country being attacked by a powerful country regarded as interference? In law there is something called an impossible condition. That is, if a country considers that it is incapable of committing a certain crime, it is enough to say: "There is no possibility that the Soviet Union will support Cuba, because there is no possibility that we will attack Cuba." But that principle was not followed. Instead the principle was established that the intervention of the Soviet Union had to be condemned.

What about the bombing of Cuba? Not a word. [*Applause*] What about the aggression against Cuba? Not a word.

Of course, there is something we should remember, which should concern us all to some extent. We are all, without any exceptions here, actors and participants in a crucial moment in the history of humanity. At times, it seems, criticism does not reach us; we are not aware of condemnation and censure for our deeds. This occurs above all when we forget that in addition to having the privilege of playing a part in this all-important moment of history, some day history itself will judge us for our acts.

In the face of the refusal to defend our country at the meeting in Costa Rica, we smile—because history itself will judge that episode. I say this without bitterness. It is difficult to condemn men; men are often the playthings of circumstance. And we, who know the history of our country and are exceptional witnesses to what our country is going through today, understand how terrible it is for a nation's economy and its very life to be subject to the economic might of a foreign country.

I need only note that my country was not defended at Costa Rica. Furthermore, there was a desire that this matter not come before the United Nations—perhaps because it was felt that it was easier to obtain a mechanical majority in the OAS. That fear is not easy to explain, since we have observed that mechanical majorities often operate in the UN as well.

With all due respect to this organization, I must state here what lessons our people have learned from this. The Cuban people are a people who have learned much, a people who we proudly say are equal to the role they are playing at this moment and to the heroic struggle they are carrying out. They have learned much in the school of these recent international events. That is why they know that in the end, when our country's rights have been denied, when the aggressive forces attack it, our people themselves have the supreme and heroic recourse of resisting when Cuba's rights are not safeguarded in either the OAS or the UN. [*Ovation*]

That is why the small countries still do not feel so certain that our rights will be preserved. That is why when the small countries want to be free we know that we are doing so on our own account and at our own risk. Because in truth the peoples, when they are united, when they defend a just cause, can rely on their own energies. It is not a matter of a handful of men—as they have tried to paint us—ruling a country. It is a matter of a whole people ruling a country, firmly united and with a great revolutionary consciousness, defending its rights. The enemies of the Cuban revolution should know this, because if they do not they are making a terrible mistake.

These are the circumstances in which the revolutionary process in Cuba has taken place. This is how we found the country and this is why the difficulties arose. And yet the Cuban revolution is changing things. What was yesterday a land without hope, a land of misery, a land of illiteracy, is beginning to become one of the most enlightened, advanced, and developed lands of this continent.

The revolutionary government, in but twenty months, has created ten thousand new schools. In this brief span of time, we have built as many schools in the countryside as had been built in the previous fifty years. Cuba is today the first country of Latin America that has all the schools it needs, that has a teacher in even the most remote corners of the mountains.

The revolutionary government, in this brief period of time, has built twenty-five thousand houses in the city and countryside. Fifty new townships are being built in our country at this moment. The most important military fortresses today house tens of thousands of students.[28]

In the coming year, our country intends to wage its great battle against illiteracy, with the ambitious goal of teaching every single illiterate person in the country to read and write. Toward that end, organizations of teachers, students, and workers—that is, the entire people—are preparing themselves for an intensive campaign. Cuba will be the first country of Latin America that, within the course of a few months, will be able to say it does not have one single illiterate person.[29]

Today our people are receiving care from hundreds of doctors who have been sent out into the rural areas to fight the endemic diseases there, the parasitic diseases, and to improve the sanitary conditions of the nation.

In another aspect, the conservation of our natural resources, we can also state here that in a single year, in the most ambitious plan for the conservation of natural resources being carried out in the hemisphere—including the United States and Canada—we have planted close to fifty million timber-yielding trees.

Youths who had no jobs or schools have been organized by the revolutionary government and are today carrying out useful work for the country, at the same time as they are being prepared for productive work.

Agricultural production in our country has registered something almost unheard-of: production has increased from the very start. From the first moment agricultural production has increased. Why did this happen? First of all, the revolutionary government turned more than 100,000 small farmers into owners of their land. At the same time it preserved large-scale production by means of agricultural production cooperatives—that is to say, large-scale production was maintained through cooperatives. As a result, we have been able to apply the most modern agricultural techniques, leading to an increase in production from the very start.

All these social programs—teachers, housing, hospitals—have been carried out without sacrificing the resources needed for development. At this moment, the revolutionary government is carrying forward a program of industrialization, and the first factories are already being built in Cuba.

We have utilized the resources of our country rationally. Previously, for example, Cuba spent $35 million importing automobiles and $5 million importing tractors. A primarily agricultural country was importing seven times more automobiles than tractors. We have turned this figure upside down, and are now importing seven times more tractors than automobiles.

Close to $500 million was recovered from the politicians who had enriched themselves under the dictatorship. The total value of what we were able to recover from the corrupt politicians who had been pillaging our country came to almost $500 million in cash and assets.

The correct investment of this wealth and these resources is what has allowed the revolutionary government to carry out a plan of industrialization and to increase agricultural production simultaneously with building houses and schools, sending teachers to the farthest corners of the country, and providing medical attention—in other words, carrying out a program of social development.

At the recently concluded Bogotá meeting, as you know, the U.S. government once again proposed a plan. But was it a plan for economic development? No, it proposed a plan for "social development."[30] What was meant by this? Well, it was a plan for building houses, schools, and roads. But does this solve the problem? How can there be a solution to the social problems without a plan for economic development? Are they trying to hoodwink the peoples of Latin America? What are the families going to live on when they inhabit those houses, if those houses are actually built? What shoes and what clothes are the children going to wear, and what food are they going to eat, when they go to those schools? Do they perhaps not know that when a family has no clothes or shoes for the children, they are not sent to school? With what resources are they going to pay the teachers? With what resources are they going to pay the doctors? With what resources are they going to pay for the medicines? If they want a good way to save on medicines they should improve the people's nutritional level, for what is spent on improving the people's nutritional level will help save money on hospitals.

Faced with the tremendous reality of underdevelopment, the U.S. government now comes up with a plan for social development. Naturally it is significant that the U.S. government is concerned with the problems of Latin America. Up to now it had not cared at all. What a coincidence that they are now concerned with these problems! And the fact that this concern has arisen after the Cuban revolution, well, they'll say this is purely accidental.

Until now the monopolies have been concerned solely with exploiting the underdeveloped countries. But as soon as the Cuban revolution arises, the monopolies are concerned about the underdeveloped countries. While with one hand the U.S. government attacks Cuba economically and tries to crush us, with the other hand it offers charity to the peoples of Latin America. It does not offer resources for economic development, which is what Latin America wants, but resources for social development. They offer resources for houses for people without work, for schools to which children cannot go, and for hospitals that would not be necessary if nutrition levels were a little better in Latin America. [Applause]

Although some of my Latin American colleagues may feel it their duty to be discreet here, they really should welcome a revolution such as the Cuban revolution, which at the minimum has forced the monopolies to return at least a small part of their profits from the natural resources and the sweat of the peoples of Latin America. [Applause]

It does not bother us that we are not included in this assistance; we do not get angry about such things. We have been solving these types of problems for a long time, problems of schools and housing and so on. Some may feel, however, that we are using this for propaganda purposes; the president of the United States said that some had come to use this rostrum to make propaganda.

Well, all of my colleagues in the United Nations have a standing invitation to visit Cuba. We do not close our doors to anyone, nor do we restrict the movements of anyone. All of my colleagues in this assembly can visit Cuba and see for themselves. You know that chapter of the Bible that speaks of St. Thomas, who had to see before he would believe—I think it was St. Thomas. Well, we can invite any journalist or any member of a delegation to visit Cuba and see what a people can do with its own resources when it invests them honestly and rationally. But we are not only solving our problems of housing and education; we are also solving the problem of development, because without solving the problem of development there can be no solution of the social problems.

But what is happening? Why does the U.S. government not wish to speak of development? Very simply because the U.S. government does not want to quarrel with the monopolies, and the monopolies need natural resources and investment markets for their capital. That is the contradiction. That is why the true solution of this problem is not sought. That is why there is no development plan for the underdeveloped countries using public investments.

This should be stated here clearly, because we, the underdeveloped countries, are after all the majority here—in case anyone does not know it. And we are, after all, witnesses to what is going on in the underdeveloped countries. The true solution is not sought and they always talk here of the contribution of private capital. Naturally this means markets for the investment of surplus capital, such as the investments that amortize in five years.

The U.S. government cannot propose a plan for public investment, because this would go against the U.S. government's very reason for existence, which is the U.S. monopolies. There is no need to beat around the bush; that is the reason why no true program of economic development is planned. The goal is to preserve the lands of Latin America, Africa, and Asia for the investment of surplus capital.

Thus far we have referred to the problems of our own country with the U.S. government, asking why they have not been solved. Is it because we did not want them solved? Hardly. The government of Cuba has always been ready to discuss its problems with the U.S. government, but the U.S. government has not wanted to discuss its problems with Cuba. It must have its reasons for not wanting to discuss these problems with Cuba.

Right here I have a note sent by the revolutionary government of Cuba to the government of the United States on January 27, 1960. It says:

The differences of opinion between the two governments that are subject to diplomatic negotiation can be settled by such negotiation. The government of Cuba is ready and willing to discuss these differences without reservation and in full detail, and declares that it does not see any obstacles in the path of such negotiations via any of the traditional means set up for these purposes, on the basis of mutual respect and reciprocal benefit. The government of Cuba wishes to maintain and increase diplomatic and economic relations between the two countries, and understands that on this basis the traditional friendship between the peoples of Cuba and the United States is indestructible.

On February 22 of this year the revolutionary government of Cuba,

in accordance with its desire to renew through diplomatic channels the negotiations already begun on issues pending between the United States of America and Cuba, has decided to set up a commission with the necessary powers to begin its efforts in Washington on a mutually agreed date.

The revolutionary government of Cuba wishes to make clear, however, that the renewal and continuance of such negotiations must necessarily be subject to the condition that the government or the Congress of your country does not take any unilateral measure prejudging the results of the above-mentioned negotiations or prejudicial to the economy or the people of Cuba.

It seems obvious to add that the adherence of the government of Your Excellency to this point of view would not only contribute to improving relations between our respective

countries but would also reaffirm the spirit of close friendship that has traditionally linked our peoples. It would also
allow both governments, in an atmosphere of calmness and
with the widest scope possible, to examine the questions that
have adversely affected the traditional relations between Cuba
and the United States of America.

What was the reply of the U.S. government?

The government of the United States cannot accept the
conditions for negotiations expressed in Your Excellency's note
to the effect that measures should not be taken of a unilateral
nature on the part of the government of the United States
that might affect the economy or people of Cuba, whether by
the legislative or the executive branch. As President Eisenhower stated on January 26, the government of the United
States of America, in the exercise of its own sovereignty, must
keep itself free to take whatever measures it deems necessary,
conscious of its international obligations to defend the legitimate rights and interests of its people.

In other words, the government of the United States does
not deign to discuss its differences with the small country of
Cuba.

What hope do the people of Cuba have for a solution of these
problems? All the facts that we have been able to observe here
conspire against a solution of these problems. The United Nations should take this very much into account, because the government and people of Cuba are justifiably concerned at the
aggressive turn in U.S. government policy regarding Cuba. It is
well that this body should know the facts.

First of all, the U.S. government considers it has the right
to promote subversion in our country. The U.S. government
is promoting the organization of subversive movements
against the revolutionary government of Cuba, a fact we
hereby denounce in this General Assembly.

Concretely we wish to denounce what has taken place on a Caribbean island that belongs to Honduras, known as the Swan Islands. The U.S. government has taken over these islands militarily; U.S. marines are there, despite the fact that this is Honduran territory, stripping a sister people of a piece of its territory.[31] And there, in violation of international law and the international conventions that govern radio broadcasting, it has set up a powerful transmitter, which it has put at the disposal of the war criminals and the subversive groups that are sheltered here in this country. In addition, military training is being given there to promote subversion and armed landings on our island.

It would be good if the representative of Honduras to the General Assembly were to assert here Honduras's right to that piece of its territory. But that is a matter incumbent upon the representative of Honduras. What is of direct concern to us is that a piece of territory belonging to a sister country, seized in a pirate-like fashion by the U.S. government, should be used as a base for subversion and attacks against our territory. I wish to denounce this act here on behalf of the government and people of Cuba.

Does the U.S. government feel it has the right to promote subversion in our country, violating all international agreements, invading our airwaves, to the great detriment of our radio stations? Does this mean then that the revolutionary government of Cuba also has the right to promote subversion in the United States? If the United States feels it has the right to intrude upon our airwaves, does this then mean that the Cuban government also has the right to intrude upon U.S. airwaves?

What right can the U.S. government have over us or over our island such that it permits itself to demand the same right over other peoples? The United States should return the Swan Islands to Honduras, because it never had jurisdiction over those islands. [*Applause*]

But there are even more alarming circumstances for our people. It is known that by virtue of the Platt Amendment, imposed on our people by force, the U.S. government proclaimed the right to establish naval bases on our territory, a right imposed by force and maintained by force.[32]

A naval base on any country's territory is surely just cause for concern. In our case, first of all, a country that has followed an aggressive and militaristic foreign policy possesses a base in the very heart of our island, thereby subjecting our island to the dangers of international conflicts, of atomic conflicts, even though we have nothing to do with them. We have nothing to do with the problems of the U.S. government, or with the crises that the U.S. government provokes. And yet there is a base in the very heart of our island that poses a danger for us in the event of an armed conflict.

But is that the only danger? By no means. There is a danger that concerns us even more, since it is closer to home. The revolutionary government of Cuba has repeatedly expressed its concern that the imperialist government of the United States might use that base within our territory to stage an attack against itself, in order to justify an attack on our country. I repeat: The revolutionary government of Cuba is greatly concerned that the imperialist government of the United States may stage an attack against its own forces as a pretext for an attack on our country. This concern on our part is increasing, because U.S. aggressiveness is increasing and the symptoms are becoming more alarming.

I have here, for example, an Associated Press dispatch, which we received:

> Admiral Arleigh Burke, U.S. Chief of Naval Operations, says that if Cuba should attempt to take the Guantánamo naval base by force "we would fight back."
>
> In a copyrighted interview published today in the magazine *U.S. News & World Report*, Admiral Burke was asked if the Navy is concerned about the situation in Cuba under Premier Fidel Castro.
>
> "Yes, our Navy is concerned—not about our base at

Guantánamo, but about the whole Cuban situation," Admiral Burke said.

—The admiral added that all the military services are concerned.

"Is that because of Cuba's strategic position in the Caribbean?" he was asked.

"Not necessarily," Admiral Burke said. "Here is a country with a people normally very friendly to the United States, people who have liked the people of this country—and we have liked them. Yet, here has come a man with a small, hard core of Communists determined to change all of that. Castro has taught hatred of the United States and he has gone far toward wrecking his country."

Admiral Burke said "we would react very fast" if Castro moved against the Guantánamo base.

"If they would try to take the place by force, we would fight back," he added.

To a question whether Soviet Premier Khrushchev's threats about retaliatory rockets give Admiral Burke "second thoughts about fighting in Cuba," the Admiral said:

"No. Because he's not going to launch his rockets. He knows he will be destroyed if he does—I mean Russia will be destroyed."

First of all, I must emphasize that for this gentleman, increasing industrial production in my country by 35 percent, giving employment to more than 200,000 Cubans, finding solutions to our country's social problems—all this is equivalent to "wrecking the country." Therefore, they take upon themselves the right to set the stage for aggression.

Notice how they calculate. And their calculation is very dangerous, since this gentleman feels that in case of an attack on us we will be alone. This is simply a calculation by Admiral Burke.

But let us imagine that Mr. Burke is mistaken. Let us imagine that Mr. Burke, even though he is a big admiral, is mistaken. In that event Admiral Burke is playing irresponsibly with the fate of the world. [*Applause*] Admiral Burke and all those of his aggressive militarist group are playing with the fate of the world.

Our individual fate is really of no concern. Yet we who represent the peoples of the world are duty-bound to concern ourselves with the fate of the world, and it is our duty to condemn all those who play irresponsibly with it. They are not playing solely with the fate of my country's people; they are also playing with the fate of their own people, and of all the peoples of the world.

Or does this Admiral Burke think that we are still living in the era of the flintlock rifle? Does this Admiral Burke not realize that we are living in the atomic age, whose disastrous destructive force could not even have been imagined by Dante or Leonardo da Vinci, with all their imagination, because it surpasses what man was ever able to imagine. And yet he makes this calculation, which AP spreads throughout the world. The magazine has just come out and already the campaign has begun. The hysteria is being whipped up and the imaginary danger of a Cuban attack against the Guantánamo base is being spread.

But that is not all. Yesterday a UPI dispatch appeared containing a declaration by U.S. Senator Styles Bridges who, as I understand it, is a member of the Senate Armed Services Committee. Senator Bridges said that "the United States must defend at all costs its naval base at Guantánamo in Cuba."

He added:

> We must go as far as necessary to preserve that base and to defend that gigantic installation of the United States. We have naval forces there; we have marines there, and if we were attacked we should certainly defend it, for I consider it to be the most important base in the Caribbean region.

This member of the Senate Armed Services Committee did not entirely discount the use of atomic weapons in the event of an attack against the base. What does this mean? This means that not only is hysteria being whipped up, not only are they systematically creating the climate, but we are even being threatened with the use of atomic weapons. One of the many things one could ask this Mr. Bridges is whether it gives him no shame to threaten a small country like Cuba with atomic weapons. [*Loud applause*]

As far as we are concerned, I must say with all due respect that the world's problems are not settled by threats or by sowing fear. And what about our small and modest nation? We exist, whether they like it or not. And the revolution will continue to go forward, whether they like it or not. Our small and modest nation must accept its fate. Our people are not frightened by their threats to use atomic weapons.

What does this mean? There are many countries that have U.S. military bases, but at least these are not directed against the governments that granted the concessions—to the best of our knowledge. Our case is more tragic because the base is located on our island, directed against Cuba and its revolutionary government. That is, it is in the hands of the declared enemies of our country, our revolution, and our people.

In the entire history of bases set up around the world, the most tragic case is that of Cuba. This base was imposed by force and is located in territory that is unmistakably ours, that is a good many miles from the coast of the United States. It is a base imposed by force that is directed against Cuba and its people, and is a constant threat and cause for concern for our people.

That is why we must state here that all this talk of attacks is intended primarily to create hysteria and to set the stage for attacks against our country. We have never said a single word that could imply any type of attack on the Guantánamo naval base, because we are the ones most interested in not wanting to give imperialism a pretext to attack us.

We state this here categorically. But we also declared it from the moment that base became a threat to the peace and security of our country and our people. The revolutionary government of Cuba is seriously considering requesting, within the framework of international law, that the naval and military forces of the U.S. government be withdrawn from that portion of our national territory. [*Loud applause*] And the imperialist government of the United States will have no other option than to withdraw its forces. How will it be able to justify before the world its right to install on territory that is unmistakably Cuban an atomic base, a base that poses a danger to our people? How will the U.S. government be able to justify to the world its right to maintain and hold sovereignty over a part of our territory? How will it be able to stand before the world and justify something so arbitrary? And since it will be unable to justify itself to the world when our government asks it to do so, then within the framework of international law, the U.S. government will have no other option than to abide by its terms.

But this assembly needs to be kept well informed on the problems of Cuba and must be alert to deception and confusion. We have to explain these problems very clearly because they involve the security and fate of our country. That is why we want these matters clearly understood—especially since there appears to be little chance of correcting the opinion, or the erroneous impression, held by U.S. politicians regarding Cuba.

I have here, for example, a few statements by Mr. Kennedy that are enough to astound anybody.[33] On Cuba he says: "We must use all the power of the OAS to prevent Castro from interfering in the affairs of other Latin American governments and to force him to return freedom to Cuba." They are going to return freedom to Cuba!

"We must make clear our intention," he says, "to not permit the Soviet Union to turn Cuba into its Caribbean base, and to apply the Monroe Doctrine." More than halfway through the twentieth century this candidate speaks of the Monroe Doctrine![34] "We must force Prime Minister Castro to understand that we intend to defend our right to the Guantánamo naval base." This is the third person to speak of this problem. "And we must show the Cuban people that we sympathize with their legitimate economic aspirations." And why did they not sympathize before? "We know their love of freedom, and we shall never be satisfied until democracy returns to Cuba." What democracy is he talking about? The democracy made by the imperialist monopolies of the U.S. government?

So that you may understand why planes fly over Cuba from U.S. territory, pay attention to what this gentleman says:

"The forces that are fighting for freedom in exile and in the mountains of Cuba must be supplied and assisted, and in other countries of Latin America communism must be confined, and not allowed to expand or spread."

If Kennedy were not an illiterate and ignorant millionaire [*Applause*] he would understand that it is not possible to carry out a revolution over the opposition of the peasants in the mountains and with the support of the landowners. Every time imperialism has tried to foment counterrevolutionary groups, the peasant militias have put them out of commission within days. But it seems he has read some novels or seen some Hollywood film about guerrilla warfare, and he believes that social forces exist to wage guerrilla warfare in Cuba today.

In any case, this is not encouraging. Nobody should think, however, that these opinions of ours on Kennedy's statements indicate any sympathy on our part for the other one, Mr. Nixon, [*Laughter*] who has made similar statements. As far as we are concerned, both of them lack political brains.

GENERAL ASSEMBLY PRESIDENT FREDERICK H. BOLAND (IRELAND): I am sorry to have to interrupt the prime minister of Cuba, but I am sure that I am faithfully reflecting the feelings of the assembly as a whole when I ask him to consider whether it is right and proper that the candidates in the current election in this country be discussed at the rostrum of the assembly of the United Nations.

I am sure that in this matter the distinguished prime minister of Cuba will, on reflection, see my point of view, and I feel that I can rely with confidence on his goodwill and cooperation. On that basis I would ask him kindly to continue with his remarks.

CASTRO: It is not our intention in the least to infringe upon the rules that determine our behavior in the United Nations, and the president can depend fully on my cooperation to avoid having my words misunderstood. I have no intention of offending anyone. It is somewhat a question of style and, above all, a question of confidence in the assembly. In any case, I will try to avoid wrong interpretations.

Up to this point we have been dealing with the problem of our country, which is the fundamental reason for our coming to the United Nations. But we understand perfectly that it would be somewhat selfish on our part to limit our concern to our specific case alone. While it is true that we have used up the greater part of our time informing this assembly about the case of Cuba, and there is not much time left, we would like to refer briefly to the remaining questions.

The case of Cuba is not an isolated one. It would be an error to think of it only as the case of Cuba. The case of Cuba is that of all underdeveloped nations. It is the case of the Congo; it is the case of Egypt; it is the case of Algeria; it is the case of Iran. [*Applause*] It is the case of Panama, which wants its canal. It is the case of Puerto Rico, whose national spirit is being suppressed. It is the case of Honduras, a portion of whose territory has been seized. In short, although we have not made reference to other countries specifically, the case of Cuba is the case of all the underdeveloped and colonized countries.

The problems we were describing concerning Cuba apply to all Latin America. Latin America's economic resources are controlled by the monopolies. If they do not directly own these resources, they exercise control in other ways. For example, they may control the mining and extraction of natural resources, as with copper in Chile, Peru, and Mexico; as with zinc in Peru and Mexico; and as with oil in Venezuela. Or they may be the owners of the public utility companies, as with the electricity companies in Argentina, Brazil, Chile, Peru, Ecuador, and Colombia; or as with the telephone companies in Chile, Brazil, Peru, Venezuela, Paraguay, and Bolivia. Or they may control the commercial sale of our products, as with coffee in Brazil, Colombia, El Salvador, Costa Rica, and Guatemala; or as with the exploitation, marketing, and transportation of bananas by the United Fruit Company in Guatemala, Costa Rica, and Honduras; or as with cotton in Mexico and Brazil. In all these cases, the monopolies exercise economic control over the most important industries of the country. These economies are completely dependent on the monopolies.

Woe to these countries on the day when they too should wish to carry out an agrarian reform! They will be asked for "speedy, efficient, and just payment." And if, in spite of everything, they do carry out an agrarian reform, the representative from this sister nation who comes to the United Nations will be confined to Manhattan; hotels will not rent to him; insults will be showered upon him; and he may even be mistreated by the police themselves.[35]

The problem of Cuba is merely an example of the condition of Latin America. How long must Latin America wait for its development? As far as the monopolies are concerned, it will have to wait until the Greek calends.[36] Who is going to industrialize Latin America—the monopolies? Certainly not.

There is a report of the United Nations Economic Commission that explains how even private investment capital, rather than going to the countries needing it most to help them set up basic industries and contribute to their development, is channeled to the more industrialized countries because there private capital finds—so it says, or believes—greater security. Naturally even the Economic Commission of the United Nations has to recognize that there is no possibility of development through investment of private capital—that is, through the monopolies.

Latin America's development will have to come through public investment, planned out and granted unconditionally, without political conditions. Obviously we would all like to represent free countries. No one likes to represent a country that does not feel itself free. No one wants the independence of his country to be subject to any interest other than its own. Therefore the assistance must be without political conditions.

The fact that Cuba was denied assistance is of no importance. We did not ask for it. However, on behalf of the peoples of Latin America we feel it our duty, out of a sense of solidarity, to state that assistance must be given without political conditions. Public investment must be for economic development, not for "social development"—which is the latest invention to hide the genuine need for economic development.

The problems of Latin America are like the problems of the rest of the underdeveloped world in Africa and Asia. The world is divided up among the monopolies. The same monopolies we see in Latin America are also seen in the Middle East. There the oil is in the hands of monopoly companies that are controlled by the financial interests of the United States, Britain, the Netherlands, and France. This is the case in Iran, Iraq, Saudi Arabia, and all corners of the world. The same thing happens in the Philippines. The same thing happens in Africa.

The world has been divided up among the monopolistic interests. Who would dare deny this historic truth? And the monopolistic interests do not want to see these nations develop. What they want is to exploit these nations' natural resources and to exploit their people. And the sooner these interests amortize their investments or get them back, so much the better.

The problems that the Cuban people have had with the imperialist government of the United States are the same problems that Saudi Arabia would have if it decided to nationalize its oil fields, or if Iran or Iraq decided to do so. These are the same problems that Egypt had when it quite justifiably nationalized the Suez Canal; these are the same problems that Indonesia had when it wanted to become independent.[37] They would face the same surprise attack that was made against Egypt; the same type of surprise attack made against the Congo.

Have the colonialists or the imperialists ever lacked pretexts to invade a country? Never! They have always managed to find some pretext. Which are the colonialist countries? Which are the imperialist countries? There are not four or five countries but four or five groups of monopolies that possess the world's wealth.

Let us imagine that a person from outer space were to come to this assembly, someone who had read neither the *Communist Manifesto* of Karl Marx nor UPI or AP dispatches or any other monopoly-controlled publication. If he were to ask how the world was divided up and he saw on a map that the wealth was divided among the monopolies of four or five countries, he would say, "The world has been badly divided up, the world has been exploited." Here in this assembly, where the underdeveloped countries make up the big majority, he could say, "The great majority of the peoples, who you represent, have been exploited for a long time. The forms of exploitation may have changed, but they continue to be exploited." That would be the verdict.

In his speech Premier Khrushchev made a statement that very much attracted our attention because of the value it holds. He said that the Soviet Union had neither colonies nor investments in any country. How great would our world be today— our world today threatened with catastrophe—if the representatives of all nations could make the same statement: Our country has neither colonies nor investments in any foreign country! [*Applause*]

Why go around and around? This is the crux of the matter. This is the crux of the question of war and peace. This is the crux of the arms race and disarmament. Since the beginning of humanity, wars have arisen for one reason and one reason alone: the desire of some to plunder the wealth of others.

End the philosophy of plunder and the philosophy of war will be ended as well. [*Applause*] End the existence of colonies and the exploitation of countries by monopolies, and humanity will have achieved a true era of progress.

Until that step is taken, until that stage is reached, the world will have to live constantly under the nightmare of being dragged into crisis, into atomic conflagration. Why? Because there are those with an interest in perpetuating plunder and because there are those with an interest in maintaining exploitation.

We have spoken here of Cuba. Our case has taught us lessons as a result of the problems we have had to confront with our own imperialism, that is, the imperialism we confront. But in fact all imperialisms are alike, and they are all allied. A country that exploits the peoples of Latin America or any part of the world is allied with those who exploit the other peoples of the world.

There was one statement made by the president of the United States that alarmed us considerably:

In the developing areas, we must seek to promote peaceful change as well as to assist economic and social progress. To do this—to assist peaceful change—the international community must be able to manifest its presence in emergencies through United Nations observers or forces.

I should like to see member countries take positive action on the suggestion in the secretary-general's report looking to the creation of a qualified staff within the Secretariat to assist him in meeting future needs for United Nations forces.

In other words, after considering Latin America, Africa, Asia, and the Pacific as "developing areas," he suggests that there be "peaceful change," and he proposes that in order to bring this about, United Nations "observers" or "forces" should be used.

The United States came into being through a revolution against its colonial rulers. The right of peoples to free themselves from colonial rule or any form of oppression by means of revolution was recognized in Philadelphia by the declaration of July 4, 1776. And yet today the U.S. government proposes to use United Nations forces to prevent revolutionary change. President Eisenhower continued:

> The secretary-general has now suggested that members should maintain a readiness to meet possible future requests from the United Nations for contributions to such forces. All countries represented here should respond to this need by earmarking national contingents which could take part in United Nations forces in case of need. The time to do it is now—at this assembly.
>
> I assure countries which now receive assistance from the United States that we favor use of that assistance to help them maintain such contingents in the state of readiness suggested by the secretary-general.

In other words, he proposes to the countries that have bases and are receiving assistance that he is ready to give them more assistance for the formation of this UN emergency force.

> To assist the secretary-general's efforts, the United States is prepared to earmark substantial air and sea transport facilities on a standby basis, to help move contingents requested by the United Nations in any future emergency.

In other words, the United States also offers its planes and ships for the use of such emergency forces. We wish to state here that the Cuban delegation does not agree with such an emergency force until all peoples of the world can feel sure that these forces will not be put at the disposal of colonialism and imperialism. [*Applause*] This is especially so inasmuch as our countries can at any moment become the victim of the use of such forces against the rights of our peoples.

There are a number of problems that have been mentioned here by various representatives. For reasons of time, we would like merely to express our opinion on the problem of the Congo.[38]

Given our stand against colonialism and against the exploitation of the underdeveloped countries, it is not surprising that we condemn the way in which the intervention by United Nations forces was carried out in the Congo. First of all, the UN forces did not go there to counter the invading forces, for which they had originally been sent. All the time necessary was given to bring about the first dissension, and when this did not suffice, further time was given enabling the second division to occur in the Congo.

Finally, while the radio stations and airfields were being occupied, further time was given for the emergence of the "third man," as such saviors who emerge in these circumstances are known. We know them all too well, because in 1934 one of these saviors also appeared in our country, named Fulgencio Batista. In the Congo his name is Mobutu. In Cuba this savior paid a daily visit to the U.S. Embassy, and it seems that in the Congo it is the same. Don't just take my word for it. No, this was published in no less than *Time* magazine, which is the biggest defender of the monopolies, and therefore cannot be against them. They cannot be in favor of Lumumba, because they are against him and in favor of Mobutu. But they explain who Mobutu is, how he went about his work, and it winds up by saying—and I'm quoting the latest issue of *Time:*

"Mobutu became a frequent visitor to the U.S. Embassy and held long talks with officials there.

"One afternoon last week, Mobutu conferred with officers at Camp Leopold, and got their cheering support. That night he went to Radio Congo"—the same station that Lumumba had not been allowed to use—"and abruptly announced that the army was taking over."

In other words, all this occurred after frequent visits and lengthy conversations with officials of the U.S. embassy. This is what *Time* magazine says, a defender of the monopolies.

In other words, the hand of the colonialist interests has been clearly visible in the Congo. Our position therefore is that bad faith has been in evidence, that favoritism was displayed toward the colonial interests, and that all the facts indicate that the people of the Congo—and justice in the Congo—are on the side of the only leader who remained there to defend the interests of his country. And that leader is Lumumba. [*Applause*]

This mysterious third man in the Congo was called upon to remove the legitimate government of the Congo, as well as trample on the legitimate interests of the Congolese people. In view of this situation, if the Afro-Asian countries manage to reconcile all these interests to the benefit of the Congo, well and good. But if this conciliation is not achieved, then justice and the law will be on the side of he who not only has the support of the people and the parliament, but is the one who stood firm against the interests of the monopolies and stood together with his people.

Regarding the problem of Algeria, I hardly have to say that we are 100 percent on the side of the right of the Algerian people to independence.[39] [*Applause*] Furthermore, like many other artificial claims of the vested interests, it is ridiculous to pretend that Algeria is part of the French nation. Similar efforts have been made by other countries to hold on to their colonies in other times. That attempt, known as integralism, was a historical failure. Let us look at the question in reverse: suppose Algeria was the colonial power and declared that part of Europe formed an integral part of its territory. This is obviously an idea that is dragged in arbitrarily, and has no meaning whatsoever. Algeria belongs to Africa, gentlemen, just as France belongs to Europe.

For a number of years this African people has been waging a heroic struggle against the colonial power. Perhaps even while we are discussing things calmly, the bombs and shells of the French government or army are falling over Algerian villages and hamlets. And men are dying in a fight where there can be no possible doubt which side is right. It is a struggle that could be settled even taking into account the interests of the French minority living there, which is used as a pretext to deny the right of independence to nine-tenths of the population of Algeria. And yet we do nothing. How quick we were to go to the Congo, and how half-hearted we are about Algeria! [*Applause*] And if the Algerian government—which is also a government because it represents millions of Algerians who are fighting— were to ask for United Nations forces to go there, would we go? And with the same enthusiasm? I wish we would go with the same enthusiasm, but with very different purposes—with the aim of defending the interests of the colony and not the interests of the colonizers.

We are thus on the side of the Algerian people, just as we are on the side of the other peoples of Africa that are still under colonial rule. We are on the side of the Blacks who suffer discrimination in the Union of South Africa. We are on the side of the peoples that wish to be not only politically free—because it is very easy to have a flag, a coat of arms, an anthem, and a color on the map—but also economically free. Because the first and most basic truth we must all bear in mind is that there can be no political independence without economic independence. Political independence is a fiction unless there is economic independence, and therefore we defend the aspiration to be economically and politically free; not just having a flag, a coat of arms, and a representative in the UN.

We want to mention another right here, a right that was proclaimed by our people at a huge public assembly a few days ago. I refer to the right of the underdeveloped countries to nationalize without compensation their natural resources and the monopoly investments in their countries.[40] In other words, we advocate the nationalization of natural resources and foreign investments in the underdeveloped countries. And if the economically developed countries wish to do likewise, we shall not oppose it. [*Applause*]

For countries to be truly free politically, they must be truly free economically. They must then be assisted. We may be asked: What about the value of the investments? And we shall ask in return: What about the value of the profits that have been extracted from the nations subjected to colonialism and underdevelopment for decades, if not centuries?

We would like to give our support to a proposal made by the head of the delegation of Ghana, namely, the proposal to rid African territory of military bases, and therefore of nuclear weapons bases. In other words, the proposal is to keep Africa free from the dangers of nuclear war. Something similar has already been done with Antarctica. Why, as we advance toward disarmament, do we not also advance toward freeing certain regions of the earth from the danger of nuclear war?

If Africa is being reborn, it is the Africa we are learning to know today, not the Africa that we were shown on the maps, not the Africa we were shown in Hollywood films and in novels, not the Africa of half-naked tribesmen carrying spears, ready to run away at their first encounter with the white hero—the white hero whose heroism increased in proportion to the number of African natives he killed. The Africa being reborn is the one that stands here today represented by leaders such as Nkrumah and Sékou Touré, or the Africa of Nasser and the Arab world.[41] That is the true Africa, the oppressed continent, the exploited continent, the continent from which millions of slaves came, the Africa that has suffered so greatly throughout its history. Toward that Africa we have a duty: to preserve it from the danger of destruction.

Let the other nations compensate! Let the West somehow compensate for all that Africa has been made to suffer by preserving it from the danger of atomic war, by declaring it a zone free from that danger. No atomic bases should be established there. Even if we are unable to do anything else, that continent should become a sanctuary where human life is preserved. [*Prolonged applause*] So we warmly support that proposal.

On the question of disarmament we entirely support the Soviet proposal.[42] We do not blush when we say here that we support the Soviet proposal. We believe it is a correct proposal, with clear and precise terms.

We have read very carefully the speech delivered here by President Eisenhower. He did not speak of disarmament, or the development of the underdeveloped countries, or the problem of the colonies. It would be worthwhile for the citizens of the United States, who are so influenced by false propaganda, to spend a minute and objectively read both the speech of the president of the United States and that of the prime minister of the Soviet Union. They could then see who is sincerely concerned about the problems of the world; they could then see who speaks in clear and sincere language; they could then see who wants disarmament and who does not want disarmament, and why.

The Soviet proposal is completely clear; it leaves nothing to be desired. Why should there be reservations when this tremendous problem has never before been so clearly discussed?

The history of the world has shown, tragically, that arms races always lead to war. Yet at no time has war entailed such a holocaust for humanity as at the present time, and therefore never has the responsibility been greater. And on this question that concerns the very existence of humanity, the Soviet delegation has presented a proposal for total and complete disarmament. What more could be asked? And if more could be asked, then ask for it! If further guarantees could be asked for, then ask for them! But the Soviet proposal could not be any more clear or precise. It cannot be rejected without assuming the historical responsibility for the danger of war and war itself.

Why should the problem be taken out of the hands of the General Assembly? Why does the delegation of the United States not want this problem to be discussed here among us all? Is it that we are undiscerning? Is it that we should be uninformed of this problem? Is it that a commission has to meet? Why not do it in the most democratic way possible? The General Assembly, all the delegates, should discuss here the problem of disarmament and everyone should lay his cards on the table, so that we may know who wants disarmament and who does not, who has a light-minded attitude toward war and who does not. We must know who is betraying humanity's aspiration to peace, for humanity must never be dragged into a holocaust because of selfish and illegitimate interests. Humanity, our peoples—not just ourselves—must be safeguarded from that holocaust, so that the product of human knowledge and intelligence does not serve to destroy humanity itself.

The Soviet delegation spoke in clear terms, and I say this objectively. I invite everyone to study those proposals and to place all their cards on the table. Above all, this is not only a question of delegations; this is a question of public opinion. The war makers and the militarists must be exposed and condemned by world public opinion. This is not just the duty of a minority; it is the duty of the world itself. The war makers and the militarists must be unmasked, and that is the task of public opinion. Not only must this be discussed in the plenary of the General Assembly; it must be discussed before the eyes of the entire world. It must be discussed in the great assembly of the world itself. For in the event of a war, those responsible will not be the only ones exterminated; hundreds of millions of totally innocent people will be exterminated. That is why measures must be taken by those of us meeting here as representatives of the world—or at least of part of it, because the world is still not completely here, and it will not be completely here until we have here the People's Republic of China.[43] [*Applause*] A quarter of the world is absent from this assembly. But those who are not absent have a duty to speak frankly and not beat around the bush.

We are dealing with a problem that is extremely serious. It is more important than the question of economic assistance and all other commitments, because this is a commitment to preserve the life of humanity. All of us have to discuss this problem, to speak about this problem, and to fight for peace—or at least to unmask the militarists and war makers.

Above all, if we of the underdeveloped countries want to have some hope that progress will be achieved, some hope that our peoples will enjoy a better standard of living, then we must struggle for peace and struggle for disarmament. With one-fifth of what the world spends on arms, development could be promoted in the underdeveloped countries at a 10 percent annual rate of growth. With one-fifth! And of course the standard of living of the peoples who live in the countries spending their resources on arms could be raised as well.

Now, what are the difficulties of disarmament? Who are the ones interested in being armed? The ones interested in being armed to the teeth are those who want to hold on to their colonies; to their monopolies; to the oil of the Middle East; to the natural resources of Latin America, Asia, and Africa. And in order to defend these interests, force is needed. You know full well that it was through force that these territories were occupied and colonized. It was through force that millions of human beings were enslaved. And it is through force that this exploitation is maintained in the world. So those who do not want disarmament are the ones who want to maintain the use of force, to maintain their control over the resources and the cheap labor of the underdeveloped countries. We promised we would speak frankly, and we must call things by their right names.

The colonialists, then, are enemies of disarmament. We will have to fight, using world public opinion, to impose disarmament on them, just as we will have to fight using world public opinion to impose on them the right of the peoples to political and economic liberation.

Another reason the monopolies are enemies of disarmament, besides the fact that they need arms to defend their interests, is that the arms race has always been good business for the monopolies. Everybody knows, for example, that the great monopolies in the United States doubled their capital during the Second World War. Like vultures, the monopolies feed on the corpses of war. And war is a business. Those for whom war is a business and an object of enrichment must be unmasked. The eyes of the world must be opened so they may see those for whom the fate of humanity is a business, for whom the danger of war is a business. This is especially pressing now that war can be so terrifying as to leave no way out for anyone.

This is a task to which we, a small underdeveloped country, invite the other small underdeveloped countries, as well as the whole Assembly, to fight for and to bring up here for discussion. We would never forgive ourselves if, whether through neglect or through a lack of firmness or energy on our part around this question, the world were to find itself increasingly facing the dangers of war.

There is one remaining point that, as I have read in some newspapers, was one of the points the Cuban delegation wanted to raise. That is the question of the People's Republic of China. A number of delegations have already spoken of this. We merely wish to state that the fact that this problem has not even been discussed here is really a negation of the UN's reason for existence and its very essence. Why has it not been brought up? Because the U.S. government does not want to discuss the matter. Why must the General Assembly of the United Nations renounce its right to discuss this problem?

In recent years, numerous countries have joined the UN. To oppose discussing the right of the People's Republic of China to be represented here—that is, 99 percent of a country of 600 million inhabitants—is to deny historical reality, the facts, and life itself. It is simply preposterous and absurd to not even discuss this matter. How long are we to play the sad role of not even discussing this question in the United Nations? Especially when, for example, the representatives of Franco's Spain are seated here. Mr. President, will you allow me to express my opinion, with all due respect, on this specific point, without offense to anybody?

GENERAL ASSEMBLY PRESIDENT BOLAND: I think it is only fair to the prime minister to make clear the position of the Chair. The Chair does not think it is in keeping with the dignity of the assembly or the decorum we like to preserve in our debates that references of a personal nature should be made to the heads of states or the heads of governments of member states of the United Nations, whether present here or not. I hope that the prime minister will consider that a fair and reasonable rule.

CASTRO: I merely wanted to make some comments on how the United Nations arose. The United Nations arose after the struggle against fascism, after tens of millions of human beings had died. Out of that struggle, which took so many lives, this organization arose as a hope. But there are some extraordinary paradoxes. While U.S. troops were dying in Guam, Guadalcanal, Okinawa, and many other islands in the Pacific, they were also dying on the Chinese mainland, fighting on the same side as those who today are denied the right to discuss their entry into the United Nations. At the same time the troops of the Blue Division were fighting in the Soviet Union to defend fascism.[44] [*Applause*] While the People's Republic of China is denied the right to discuss its case in the United Nations, the regime born of German nazism and Italian fascism, which took power thanks to Hitler's armies and Mussolini's Blackshirts, was generously admitted to the United Nations.

China represents one-fourth of the world. Which government is the true representative of the largest nation in the world? None other than the government of the People's Republic of China. And yet another regime maintains that seat, a regime kept in power by the interference of the U.S. Seventh Fleet in the midst of a civil war.[45]

May we ask here by what right the fleet of an extracontinental country can interfere in a purely internal affair of China—and let us repeat the term *extracontinental*, since so much has been said here of extracontinental interference. This intervention was carried out with the sole purpose of maintaining there a group of U.S. allies and preventing the total liberation of China. And since this is an absurd and illegal position from all points of view, the U.S. government does not want to discuss the problem of the People's Republic of China.

We want to make known our point of view and our support for a discussion of this problem here. We believe the General Assembly of the United Nations should seat the legitimate representatives of the Chinese people, the government of the People's Republic of China.

I understand very well that it is a bit difficult for anyone here not to be judged according to the stereotyped concepts used to judge the representatives of nations. I must state, however, that we came here free of all prejudice, to analyze problems objectively, without fear of what others might think and without fear of the consequences of our stance. We have been honest and frank—without being Francoist, [*Applause*] because we do not want to be accomplices of that injustice committed against the many Spaniards who have been imprisoned in Spain for more than twenty years and who fought together with the North Americans of the Lincoln Brigade, comrades of the same North Americans who went to Spain to raise high the name of that great North American, Abraham Lincoln.[46]

We would like to sum up our views on certain aspects of these world problems about which there can be no doubt. And in doing so we shall place our trust in reason and honesty.

We have presented here the problem of Cuba, which is part of the problem of the world. Those who attack us today are those who help attack others elsewhere in the world.

The government of the United States cannot be on the side of the Algerian people, because it is an ally of France. It cannot be on the side of the Congolese people, because it is an ally of Belgium. It cannot be on the side of the Spanish people, because it is an ally of Franco. It cannot be on the side of the Puerto Rican people, whose nationality it has been suppressing for fifty years. It cannot be on the side of the Panamanian people, who are demanding their canal. It cannot be on the side of the expansion of civilian rule in Latin America, nor in Germany or Japan.

The government of the United States cannot be on the side of peasants who want land, because it is an ally of the landowners. It cannot be on the side of workers anywhere in the world who demand better living conditions, because it is an ally of the monopolies. It cannot be on the side of colonies that want to free themselves, because it is an ally of the colonizing powers.

In other words, the government of the United States is on the side of Franco. It is on the side of the colonizers of Algeria. It is on the side of the colonizers of the Congo. It is on the side of maintaining its privileges and interests in the Panama Canal. It is on the side of colonialism all over the world.

The government of the United States is on the side of German militarism and its resurgence. It is on the side of Japanese militarism and its resurgence.

The government of the United States forgets the millions of Jews who died in the concentration camps of Europe at the hands of the Nazis, who are today recovering their influence in the German army. It forgets the French who were murdered in their heroic struggle against the German occupation. It forgets the U.S. soldiers who died at the Siegfried Line, in the Ruhr, on the Rhine, and on the battlefields of Asia.

The government of the United States cannot be on the side of the unity and the sovereignty of the peoples. Why not? Because it needs to suppress the sovereignty of the peoples in order to maintain its military bases. Each base is a dagger stuck into the sovereignty of a nation; each base is a sovereignty suppressed. That is why the U.S. government must oppose the sovereignty of the peoples. It must constantly suppress this sovereignty in order to maintain its policy of bases encircling the Soviet Union.

We understand that these problems have not been clearly explained to the people of the United States. But they should imagine how they would feel if the Soviet Union began to set up a belt of atomic bases in Cuba, in Mexico, or in Canada. The population would certainly not feel calm or secure.

World opinion, including in the United States, has to be taught to understand problems from another point of view, that of the other countries. The underdeveloped nations must not always be presented as aggressors; the revolutionaries must not always be presented as aggressors, as enemies of the people of the United States.

We cannot be enemies of the people of the United States, because we have seen North Americans such as Carleton Beals and Waldo Frank, and illustrious and distinguished intellectuals like them, who weep at the thought of the errors that are committed, at the lack of hospitality shown toward us in particular.[47] There are many North Americans—including the most humane, progressive, and courageous writers—in whom I see the same noble qualities held by the early leaders of this country, by Washington, Jefferson, and Lincoln.

I am not speaking demagogically; I am speaking with the sincere admiration that we feel for those who fought to free their people from their colonial status, so that their country would always defend noble and just ideals. They did not fight so that this country would become, as it is today, the ally of all the world's reactionaries, all the world's gangsters, the big landowners, the monopolies, the militarists, and the fascists. They did not fight so that their country would be the ally of the world's most retrograde and reactionary forces.

We know full well what the people of the United States will be told about us to keep them deceived. But no matter. We are fulfilling our duty to express these views in this historic assembly.

We proclaim the right of the peoples to their territorial integrity, to their nationality. Those who conspire against nationalism do so because they know it means the desire of the peoples to recover what belongs to them, their wealth, their natural resources.

In short, we support all the noble aspirations of all peoples. That is our position. We are and always will be on the side of the just. We are against colonialism, against exploitation, against the monopolies, against militarism, against the arms race, and against a light-minded attitude toward war. That is and always will be our position.

In conclusion, we consider it our duty to bring to the attention of this assembly the essential part of the Declaration of Havana.[48] You are aware that the Declaration of Havana was the reply of the people of Cuba to the Declaration of Costa Rica. It was not a gathering of ten, or a hundred, or a hundred thousand; it was an assembly of more than a million Cubans. Those who doubt it can go and count them at the next mass rally, or general assembly, that we hold in Cuba. You will surely see the spectacle of a fervent and conscious people, which you will most certainly not have seen elsewhere. It is a sight that one can see only when the people are ardently defending their most sacred interests.

At that assembly, in reply to the Declaration of Costa Rica, the people were consulted and they proclaimed by acclamation the following principles of the Cuban revolution:

> The National General Assembly of the People condemns the backward, inhuman latifundiary system of agricultural production, a source of misery and poverty for the rural population. It condemns starvation wages and the grossly unjust exploitation of human labor by illegitimate and privileged interests. It condemns illiteracy, the lack of teachers, schools, doctors, hospitals, and care for the elderly that prevails in Latin America. It condemns the discrimination against Blacks and Indians. It condemns the inequality and exploitation of women. It condemns the military and political oligarchies that keep our peoples in utter misery and hinder the development toward democracy and the full exercise of their sovereignty. It condemns the handing over of our countries' natural resources to the foreign monopolies as a give-away policy that betrays the interests of the peoples. It condemns the governments that ignore the feelings of their people while yielding to foreign dictates. It condemns the systematic deception of the people by the news media in the interests of the oligarchies and the imperialist oppressor. It condemns the news monopoly by the instruments of the monopoly trusts and their agents. It condemns the repressive laws that seek to prevent workers, peasants, students, and intellectuals—the great majority of each country—from organizing to fight for their social de-

mands and patriotic aspirations. It condemns the monopolies and imperialist companies that continuously plunder our wealth, exploit our workers and peasants, bleed our economies and keep them in backwardness, and force Latin American politics to submit to their designs and interests.

To sum up, the National General Assembly of the People of Cuba condemns the exploitation of man by man, and the exploitation of the underdeveloped countries by imperialist finance capital.

Therefore, the National General Assembly of the People of Cuba proclaims before the Americas:

—And we do so here before the world:

The right of peasants to the land; the right of workers to the fruit of their labor; the right of children to education; the right of the sick to medical and hospital care; the right of young people to a job; the right of students to free education that is both practical and scientific; the right of Blacks and Indians to "the full dignity of man"; the right of women to civil, social, and political equality; the right of the elderly to a secure old age; the right of intellectuals, artists, and scientists to use their work to fight for a better world; the right of nations to nationalize the imperialist monopolies, thereby recovering their national wealth and resources; the right of countries to engage freely in trade with all the peoples of the world; the right of nations to their full sovereignty; the right of the peoples to turn fortresses into schools, and to arm their workers . . .

—Because on this question we must indeed engage in an arms buildup. We must arm our people to defend ourselves from imperialist attack.

. . . and to arm their workers, peasants, students, intellectuals, Blacks, Indians, women, young people, old people, and all the oppressed and exploited, so they themselves may defend their rights and their destiny.

Some wanted to know the line followed by the revolutionary government of Cuba. All right, that is our line! [*Ovation*]

Freedom of competition or 'A free fox among free chickens'?

Ernesto Che Guevara

The United Nations sponsored a Conference on Trade and Development in Geneva, Switzerland, from March 23 to June 16, 1964, attended by delegations from 116 governments. The holding of such a conference was proposed by the First Summit Conference of Non-aligned Countries in 1961[49] primarily as a platform for the governments of the Third World countries to put forward their demands. At the conference itself, the seventy-seven underdeveloped countries in attendance formed a bloc that became known as the Group of 77, which has since grown to include over 120 countries.

The results of the Geneva meeting were discussed at the Second Summit Conference of Nonaligned Countries in October 1964. "While the Geneva Conference . . . offers a sound basis for progress in the future, the results achieved were neither adequate for, nor commensurate with the essential requirements of developing countries," stated the main resolution adopted at the Nonaligned meeting.

Coming out of the Geneva meeting, the United Nations Conference on Trade and Development (UNCTAD) was established as a permanent organ of the UN General Assembly, holding sessions every three-to-four years.

As minister of industry and a central leader of the revolutionary government, Ernesto Che Guevara was assigned to head the Cuban delegation during the opening weeks of the Geneva conference, where he delivered this address.

Ernesto Che Guevara

Freedom of competition or 'A free fox among free chickens'?

*Address to Geneva Trade and
Development Conference
March 25, 1964*

Mr. President;
Distinguished delegates:

This is the delegation of Cuba speaking, an island country situated at the mouth of the Gulf of Mexico in the Caribbean Sea. It is addressing you under the protection of its right to come to this forum and proclaim the truth. It addresses you, first of all, as a country that is going through the gigantic experience of building socialism. It does so also as a country belonging to the group of Latin American nations, even though illegal decisions have temporarily severed it from the regional organization, owing to the pressure exerted and the action taken by the United States of America.[50] Its geography indicates it is an underdeveloped country that addresses you, one that bears the scars of colonialist and imperial exploitation and that knows from bitter experience the subjugation of its markets and its entire economy or—what amounts to the same thing—the subjugation of its entire governmental machinery to a foreign power. Cuba also addresses you as a country under attack.

All these features have given our country a prominent place in the news throughout the world, despite our small size, our lack of economic importance, and our limited population.

At this conference, Cuba will express its views from the various standpoints that correspond to its particular situation in the world. But we will base our analysis on our most important and positive attribute: that of a country building socialism. As a Latin American and underdeveloped country, we will support the main demands of our sister countries, and as a country under attack we will denounce from the very outset all the schemes being cooked up by the coercive machinery of that imperialist power, the United States of America.

We preface our statement with these words of explanation because our country considers it imperative to define exactly the scope of the conference, its meaning, and its possible importance.

We come to this meeting seventeen years after the Havana conference, whose aim was to create a world order suited to the competitive interests of the imperialist powers.[51] Although Cuba was the site of that conference, our revolutionary government does not consider itself bound in the slightest by the role then played by a government subordinated to imperialist interests. Nor do we feel bound by the content or scope of the so-called Havana Charter.

At that conference, and at the previous meeting at Bretton Woods,[52] a number of international bodies were set up whose activities have been harmful to the interests of the dependent countries of the contemporary world. And even though the United States of America did not ratify the Havana Charter because it considered it too "daring," the various international credit and financial bodies and the General Agreement on Tariffs and Trade (GATT)—the tangible outcome of those two meetings—have proved to be effective weapons for defending U.S. interests.[53] What is more, they have been weapons for attacking our countries. These are subjects we will deal with at length later on.

Today, the conference agenda is broader and more realistic because it includes, among others, three of the crucial problems facing the modern world: the relations between the camp of the socialist countries and that of the developed capitalist countries, the relations between the underdeveloped countries and the developed capitalist powers, and the great problem of development for the dependent world.

The participants at this new meeting far outnumber those who met at Havana in 1947. Nevertheless, we cannot say with complete accuracy that this is a forum of the world's peoples. As a result of the strange legal interpretations that certain powers still use with impunity, countries of great importance in the world are missing from this meeting: for example the People's Republic of China, the sole lawful representative of the most populous nation on earth, whose seats are occupied by a delegation that falsely claims to represent that nation and that, to add to the anomaly, even enjoys the right of veto in the United Nations.[54]

It should also be noted that delegations representing the Democratic Republic of Korea and the Democratic Republic of Vietnam, the genuine governments of those nations, are absent, while representatives of the governments of the southern parts of both those divided states are present. To add to the absurdity of the situation, while the German Democratic Republic is unjustly excluded, the Federal Republic of Germany is attending this conference and is given a vice presidency. And while the socialist republics I mentioned are not represented here, the government of the Union of South Africa, which violates the United Nations Charter with the inhuman and fascist policy of apartheid embodied in its laws, and which defies the United Nations by refusing to transmit information on the territories that it holds in trust,[55] makes bold to occupy a seat in this hall. [*Applause*]

Because of all these anomalies, this conference cannot be

defined as the forum of the world's peoples. It is our duty to point this out and draw it to the attention of those present. Because so long as this situation persists and justice remains the tool of a few powerful interests, legal interpretations will continue to be tailored to the convenience of the oppressor powers and it will be difficult to ease the prevailing tension: a situation that entails real dangers for humanity. We also stress these facts in order to call attention to the responsibilities incumbent upon us and to the consequences that may flow from the decisions taken here. A single moment of weakness, wavering, or compromise may discredit us in the eyes of history, just as we member states of the United Nations are in a sense accomplices and, in a manner of speaking, bear on our hands the blood of Patrice Lumumba, Congolese prime minister, who was shamefully murdered at a time when United Nations troops supposedly guaranteed the stability of his government.[56] What is worse, those troops had been expressly called in by the martyr, Patrice Lumumba. Events of such gravity or of a similar nature, or that have negative implications for international relations and jeopardize our standing as sovereign nations, must not be allowed to happen at this conference.

We live in a world that is deeply and antagonistically divided into groupings of nations very dissimilar in economic, social, and political outlook. In this world of contradictions, the one existing between the socialist countries and the developed capitalist countries is spoken of as the fundamental contradiction of our time. The fact that the Cold War, conceived by the West, has shown itself lacking in real effectiveness and in political realism is one of the factors that have led to the convening of this conference. While that is the most important contradiction, however, it is nevertheless not the only one. There is also the contradiction between the developed capitalist countries and the world's underdeveloped nations. And at this conference on trade and development, the contradictions existing between these groups of nations are also of fundamental importance. In addition there is the inherent contradiction between the various developed capitalist countries, which struggle unceasingly among themselves to divide up the world and to gain stable possession of its markets so that they may enjoy substantial development based, unfortunately, on the hunger and exploitation of the dependent world.

These contradictions are important. They reflect the realities of the planet today, and they give rise to the danger of new conflagrations that, in the nuclear age, may spread throughout the world.

If, at this egalitarian conference—where all nations can express, through their votes, the hopes of their peoples—a solution satisfactory to the majority can be reached, a unique step will have been taken in the history of the world. There are many forces at work to prevent this from happening, however. The responsibility for the decisions to be taken falls on the representatives of the underdeveloped peoples. If all the peoples who live under precarious economic conditions and who depend on foreign powers for some vital aspects of their economy and for their economic and social structure are capable of resisting—coolly, although in the heat of the moment—the temptations offered them and imposing a new type of relationship here, then humanity will have taken a step forward.

If, on the other hand, the groups of underdeveloped countries, lured by the siren song of the interests of the developed powers who profit from their backwardness, compete futilely among themselves for crumbs from the tables of the world's mighty, and break the unity of numerically superior forces; or if they are not capable of insisting on clear agreements, without escape clauses open to capricious misinterpretations; or if they rest content with agreements that can simply be violated at will by the powerful, then our efforts will have been to no avail and the lengthy deliberations at this conference will result in nothing more than innocuous documents and files for the international bureaucracy to guard zealously: tons of printed paper and kilometers of magnetic tape recording the opinions expressed by the participants. And the world will stay as it is.

Such is the nature of this conference. It will have to deal not only with the problems involved in the domination of markets and the deterioration in the terms of trade but also with the main cause of this state of world affairs: the subordination of the national economies of the dependent countries to other, more developed countries that, through investments, hold sway over the main sectors of each economy.

It must be clearly understood, and we say it in all frankness, that the only way to solve the problems now besetting humanity is to eliminate completely the exploitation of dependent countries by developed capitalist countries, with all the consequences that implies. We have come here fully aware that what is involved is a discussion among the representatives of countries that have put an end to the exploitation of man by man, representatives of countries that maintain such exploitation as their guiding philosophy, and representatives of the majority group consisting of the exploited countries. We must begin our discussion by affirming the truth of these statements.

But though our convictions are so firm that no arguments can change them, we are ready to join in constructive debate in the framework of peaceful coexistence between countries with different political, economic, and social systems. The difficulty lies in making sure that we all know how much we can hope to get without having to take it by force, and where to yield a privilege before it is inevitably wrung from us by force. The conference has to proceed along this narrow, difficult path. If we stray, we shall find ourselves on barren ground.

We announced at the beginning of this statement that Cuba would speak here also as a country under attack. The latest developments, which have made our country the target of imperialist wrath and the object of every conceivable kind of repression and violation of international law, from before Playa Girón until now, are known to all.[57] It was no accident that Cuba was the main scene of one of the acts that has most seriously endangered world peace, as a result of a legitimate action taken by Cuba in exercise of its right to adopt its own principles for its people's development.[58]

Acts of aggression by the United States against Cuba began virtually as soon as the revolution triumphed. In the first stage, they took the form of direct attacks on Cuban centers of production. Later, these acts took the form of measures aimed at paralyzing the Cuban economy. About the middle of 1960 an attempt was made to deprive Cuba of the fuel needed to operate its industries, transport, and power stations. Under pressure from the State Department, the independent United States oil companies refused to sell petroleum to Cuba or to provide Cuba with tankers to ship it in. Shortly afterward, efforts were made to deprive Cuba of the foreign exchange needed for its foreign trade. A cut of 700,000 tons in the Cuban sugar quota in the United States was made by then President Eisenhower on July 6, 1960, and the quota was abolished altogether on March 31, 1961, a few days after the announcement of the Alliance for Progress[59] and a few days before Playa Girón. In an effort to paralyze Cuban industry by cutting off its supplies of raw materials and spare machine parts, the United States Commerce Department issued an order on October 19, 1960, prohibiting the shipment of a large number of products to our island. This ban on trade with Cuba was progressively intensified until on February 3, 1962, the late President Kennedy placed an embargo on all United States trade with Cuba.

After all these acts of aggression had failed, the United States went on to subject our country to an economic blockade whose purpose was to stop trade between other countries and our own. First, on January 24, 1962, the United States Treasury Department announced a ban on the importation into the United States of any article made in whole or in part from products of Cuban origin, even if it was manufactured in another country. A further step, equivalent to setting up a virtual economic blockade, was taken on February 6, 1963, when the White House issued a statement announcing that after January 1 of that year goods bought with U.S. government funds would not be shipped in vessels flying the flag of foreign countries that had traded with Cuba. This was the beginning of the blacklist, which now includes more than 150 ships belonging to countries that have not yielded to the illegal Yankee blockade. A further measure to obstruct Cuba's trade was taken on July 8, 1963, when the United States Treasury Department froze all Cuban property in the United States and prohibited the transfer of dollars to or from Cuba, together with any other kind of dollar transaction carried out through third countries.

—Mr. President, would it not be possible to ask that the disturbance be stopped, which is making it difficult to hear?—

Obsessed with the desire to attack us, the United States specifically excluded our country from the supposed benefits of the Trade Expansion Act.[60]

Acts of aggression have continued this year. On February 18, 1964, the United States announced the suspension of its aid to Great Britain, France, and Yugoslavia because these countries were still trading with Cuba. Dean Rusk, the secretary of state, said, according to the text that appeared in the U.S. newspapers: "At the same time there can be no improvement in relations with Communist China as long as that country incites and supports acts of aggression in Southeast Asia, or in those with Cuba as long as it represents a threat to the Western Hemisphere. That threat can be ended to Washington's satisfaction only with the overthrow of the Castro regime by the Cuban people. We regard that regime as temporary."

Cuba calls on the delegation of the United States government to say whether the actions foreshadowed by this statement and others like it, and the incidents we have described, are or are not at odds with coexistence in the world today, and whether, in the opinion of that delegation, the series of acts of economic aggression committed against our island and against other countries that trade with us are legitimate. I ask whether that attitude is or is not at odds with the principle of the organization that brings us together—that of practicing tolerance among states—and with the obligation imposed by that organization on countries that have ratified its charter to settle their disputes by peaceful means. I ask whether that attitude is or is not at odds with the spirit of this meeting in favor of abandoning all forms of discrimination and removing the barriers between countries with different social systems and at different stages of development. And we ask this conference to pass judgment on any explanation the United States delegation ventures to make. We, for our part, maintain the only position we have ever taken in the matter: we are ready to join in discussions provided that no prior conditions are imposed.

The period that has elapsed since the Havana Charter was signed has been marked by events of undeniable importance in the field of trade and economic development. In the first place, we have to note the expansion of the socialist camp and the collapse of the colonial system. Many countries, covering an area of more than 30 million square kilometers and with one-third of the world's population, have chosen as their system of development the construction of the communist society and, as their guiding philosophy, Marxism-Leninism. Others, without directly embracing the Marxist-Leninist philosophy, have stated their intention of laying the foundations on which to build socialism. Europe, Asia, and now Africa and Latin America are continents shaken by the new ideas abroad in the world.

The socialist camp has developed uninterruptedly at rates of growth much faster than those of the capitalist countries despite having started out, as a general rule, from fairly low levels of development and of having had to withstand wars of extermination and rigorous blockades.

In contrast to the rapid rate of growth of the countries in the socialist camp and to the development taking place, albeit much more slowly, in the majority of the capitalist countries, the unquestionable fact is that a large proportion of the so-called underdeveloped countries are in total stagnation, and in some of them the rate of economic growth is lower than that of its population increase.

These characteristics are not accidental. They are strictly in keeping with the nature of the developed capitalist system in the process of expansion, which transfers to the dependent countries the most abusive and naked forms of exploitation.

Since the end of the last century, this aggressive expansionist trend has been manifested in countless attacks on various countries in the more backward continents. Today, however, it mainly takes the form of control exercised by the developed powers over the production of and trade in raw materials in the dependent countries. In general, it is shown by the dependence of a given country on a single primary commodity, which sells only in a specific market in quantities restricted to the needs of that market.

The penetration of capital from the developed countries is the essential condition for this economic dependence. This penetration takes various forms: loans granted on onerous terms; investments that place a given country under the power of the investors; almost total technological subordination of the dependent country to the developed country; control of a country's foreign trade by the big international monopolies; and in extreme cases, the use of force as an economic power to reinforce the other forms of exploitation.

Sometimes this penetration of capital takes very subtle forms, such as the use of international financial, credit, and other types of organizations. The International Monetary Fund, the International Bank for Reconstruction and Development, GATT, and in Latin America, the Inter-American Development Bank are examples of international organizations placed at the service of the great capitalist colonialist powers—fundamentally, United States imperialism. These organizations inject themselves into domestic economic policy, foreign trade policy, and all kinds of internal financial relations as well as financial relations among different nations.

The International Monetary Fund is the watchdog of the dollar in the capitalist camp; the International Bank for Reconstruction and Development is the instrument for the penetration of United States capital into the underdeveloped world; and the Inter-American Development Bank performs the same sorry function in Latin America. All these organizations are governed by rules and principles that are represented as safeguards of fairness and reciprocity in international economic relations. In reality, however, they are merely fetishes behind which hide the most subtle instruments for the perpetuation of backwardness and exploitation. The International Monetary Fund, which is supposed to watch over the stability of exchange rates and the liberalization of international payments, merely denies the underdeveloped countries even the slightest measures of defense against competition and penetration by foreign monopolies.

The IMF imposes so-called austerity programs and opposes the forms of payment necessary for the expansion of trade between countries facing a balance-of-payments crisis and suffering from severe discriminatory measures in international trade. At the same time it strives desperately to rescue the dollar from its precarious situation without going to the heart of the structural problems afflicting the international monetary system, which block a more rapid expansion of world trade.

GATT, for its part, by establishing equal treatment and reciprocal concessions between developed and underdeveloped countries, helps to maintain the status quo and serves the interests of the former group of countries. Its machinery fails to provide the necessary means for eliminating agricultural protectionism, subsidies, tariffs, and other obstacles to the expansion of exports from the dependent countries. For all that, it now has its so-called Program of Action and, by a rather suspicious coincidence, the "Kennedy Round" is just about to begin.

In order to strengthen imperialist domination, the establishment of preferential areas has been adopted as a means of exploitation and neocolonial control. We are well acquainted with this, for we ourselves have suffered the effects of Cuban–United States preferential agreements, which shackled our trade and placed it at the disposal of the U.S. monopolies.

There is no better way to show what those preferences meant for Cuba than to quote the views of Sumner Welles, the United States ambassador [to Cuba], on the Reciprocal Trade Agreement, which was negotiated in 1933 and signed in 1934:

> The Cuban government in turn would grant us a practical monopoly of the Cuban market for American imports, the sole reservation being that in view of the fact that Great Britain was Cuba's chief customer for that portion of sugar exports which did not go to the United States the Cuban government would desire to concede certain advantages to a limited category of imports from Great Britain. . . .
>
> Finally, the negotiation at this time of a reciprocal trade agreement with Cuba along the lines above-indicated, will not only revivify Cuba but will give us practical control of a market we have been steadily losing for the past ten years not only for our manufactured products but for our agricultural exports as well notably in such categories as wheat, animal fats, meat products, rice, and potatoes.

This is a telegram from Ambassador Welles to the U.S. secretary of state, sent May 13, 1933, and published on pages 289 and 290 of volume V of the official publication, *Foreign Relations* of the United States, from 1933.

The results of the so-called Reciprocal Trade Agreement confirmed the view of Ambassador Welles.

Our country had to try to sell its main product, sugar, all over the world in order to obtain foreign currency with which to achieve a balance of payments with the United States. The special tariffs that were imposed prevented producers in European countries, as well as our own national producers, from competing with those of the United States.

It is necessary to quote only a few figures to prove that it was Cuba's function to seek foreign currency all over the world for the United States. During the period 1948–57, Cuba had a consistently unfavorable balance of trade with the United States, totaling 382.7 million pesos, whereas its trade balance with the rest of the world was consistently favorable, totaling 1.2746 billion pesos.

The balance of payments for the period 1948–58 tells the story even more eloquently: Cuba had a positive balance of 543.9 million pesos with countries other than the United States, but lost this to its rich neighbor, with whom it had a negative balance of 952.1 million pesos, with the result that its foreign currency reserves were reduced by 408.2 million pesos.

The so-called Alliance for Progress is another clear demonstration of the fraudulent methods used by the United States to maintain false hopes among nations while exploitation grows worse.

When Fidel Castro, our prime minister, pointed out at Buenos Aires in 1959 that a minimum of $3 billion a year of additional outside income was needed to finance a rate of development that would really reduce the enormous gap separating Latin America from the developed countries, many thought that the figure was exaggerated. At Punta del Este, however, $2 billion a year was promised.[61] Today, it is recognized that merely to offset the loss caused by the deterioration in the terms of trade in 1961 (the last year for which figures are available), 30 percent a year more than the hypothetical funds promised will be required. The paradoxical situation now is that while the loans are either not forthcoming or are made for projects that contribute little or nothing to the industrial development of the region, increased amounts of foreign exchange are being transferred to the industrialized countries. This means that the wealth created by the labor of peoples who live for the most part in conditions of backwardness, hunger, and poverty is enjoyed by the capitalist circles.

In 1961, for instance, according to figures given by the [United Nations] Economic Commission for Latin America, $1.735 billion left Latin America in the form of interest on foreign investments and similar payments, and $1.456 billion left in payments on foreign short-term and long-term loans. If we add to this the indirect loss of purchasing power of exports (or deterioration in the terms of trade), which amounted to $2.66 billion in 1961, and $349 million for the flight of capital, we arrive at a total of $6.2 billion, or more than three Alliances for Progress a year. Thus, assuming that the situation has not deteriorated further in 1964, the Latin American countries participating in the Alliance for Progress will lose, directly or indirectly, during the three months of this conference, almost $1.6 billion of the wealth created by the labor of their peoples.[62] On the other hand, of the $2 billion pledged for the entire year, barely half can be expected, at an optimistic estimate, to be forthcoming.

Latin America's experience with the real results of this type of "aid," which is represented as the surest and most effective means of increasing foreign earnings—better than doing it directly by increasing the volume and value of exports, and modifying their structure—has been a sad one. For this very reason it may serve as a lesson for other regions and for the underdeveloped world in general. At present our region is virtually at a standstill so far as growth is concerned. Moreover, it is devastated by inflation and unemployment, it is caught up in the vicious circle of foreign indebtedness, and it is racked with tensions that are sometimes resolved by armed conflict.

Cuba has exposed these facts as they emerged, and has predicted the outcome, while rejecting any implications in doing so other than those flowing from our example and our moral support. The development of events has proven us to be correct. The Second Declaration of Havana is proving its historical validity.[63]

These phenomena, which we have analyzed in relation to Latin America but which are valid for the whole of the dependent world, have the effect of enabling the developed powers to maintain trade conditions that lead to a deterioration in the terms of trade between the dependent countries and the developed countries.

This aspect—one of the more obvious ones, which the capi-

Above, Castro addressing
UN General Assembly,
September 26, 1960.
Right, Guevara speaking to
General Assembly,
December 11, 1964.

Above: Arriving at New York's Idlewild (now Kennedy) Airport, Castro responds to harassment by New York City police. Also in car are Raúl Roa (back seat) and Antonio Núñez.

Right: Waving to a crowd of supporters outside the Shelburne Hotel in mid-town Manhattan. In the photograph are Castro, Ramiro Valdés, Celia Sánchez, unidentified, and Antonio Núñez.

Right, an enthusiastic crowd greets the Cuban delegation outside the Hotel Theresa in Harlem. *Below,* Malcolm X meets with Castro to welcome the Cuban delegation to Harlem.

CARL NESFIELD

Above, Cubans demonstrate in Havana October 25, 1959, to protest U.S.-backed air attacks.

Right, Cuban farmers receive title to the land following passage of the agrarian reform law in 1959.

PHOTOS: RAÚL CORRALES

Right, Patrice Lumumba, seated, Congolese independence fighter and the country's first president. Speaking to the General Assembly in 1964, Guevara sharply condemned the role of UN troops in Lumumba's assassination in 1961. *Below,* demonstrators picket the UN to protest its role in the Congo, September 1960.

UNITED NATIONS

KLYTUS SMITH

Guevara at UN, December 1964. Beside him at bottom is Fernando Alvarez Tabio, Cuba's permanent UN representative.

Castro at UN,
October 1979.
Above, with UN
Secretary-General
Kurt Waldheim and
Maurice Bishop,
prime minister of
Grenada.

Top, demonstrators at UN demand an end to U.S. embargo against Cuba, 1979.
Bottom, Cuba's permanent representative Ricardo Alarcón at Security Council debate, September 25, 1990. Cuba led the fight in the Security Council to stop the U.S.-organized war against Iraq from being carried out under the banner of the United Nations.

talist propaganda machinery has been unable to conceal—is another of the factors that have led to the convening of this conference.

The deterioration in the terms of trade is quite simple in its practical effect: the underdeveloped countries must export more raw materials and primary commodities in order to import the same amount of industrial goods. The problem is particularly serious in the case of the machinery and equipment that are essential to agricultural and industrial development.

Many underdeveloped countries, on analyzing their troubles, arrive at what seems a logical conclusion. They say that if the deterioration of the terms of trade is an objective reality and the cause of most of their problems, and if it is attributable to the fall in the prices of raw materials that they export and the rise in the prices of manufactured goods that they import on the world market, then, in the case of trade relations with the socialist countries based on existing market prices, the latter will also benefit from this situation since they are, in general, exporters of manufactured goods and importers of raw materials.

We should honestly and bravely answer that this is true, but with the same honesty we must also recognize that the socialist countries have not caused the present situation. They absorb barely 10 percent of the underdeveloped countries' primary commodity exports to the rest of the world. For historical reasons they have been compelled to trade under the conditions prevailing in the world market, which is the outcome of imperialist domination over the internal economy and external markets of the dependent countries. This is not the basis on which the socialist countries establish their long-term trade with the underdeveloped countries. There are many examples to bear this out, Cuba in particular. When our social status changed and our relations with the socialist camp attained a new level of mutual trust, we did not cease to be underdeveloped, but we established a new type of relationship with the countries in that camp. The highest expression of this new relationship is the sugar price agreements we have concluded with the Soviet Union, under which that sister nation has undertaken to purchase increasing amounts of our main product at fair and stable prices until the year 1970.

Furthermore, we must not forget that there are underdeveloped countries in different circumstances and that they maintain different policies toward the socialist camp. There are some, such as Cuba, that have chosen the path of socialism; there are some that are developing in a more or less capitalist manner and are beginning to produce manufactured goods for export; there are some that have neocolonial ties; there are some that have a virtually feudal structure; and there are others that, unfortunately, do not participate in conferences of this type because the developed countries have not granted the independence to which their peoples aspire. Such is the case of British Guiana, Puerto Rico, and other countries in Latin America, Africa, and Asia. Except for the first of these categories, foreign capital has made its way into these countries in one way or another.

The demands that are today being directed to the socialist countries should be dealt with on a real basis of dialogue. In some cases this means a dialogue between underdeveloped and developed country. Almost always, however, it means a dialogue between one country subject to discrimination and another in the same situation. On many occasions, these same countries demand unilateral preferential treatment from all the developed countries without exception, including the socialist countries in this category and putting all kinds of obstacles in the way of direct trade with them. There is a danger that, by seeking to trade through their national subsidiaries, companies from the imperialist powers could be given the opportunity to make spectacular profits by claiming that a given country is underdeveloped and therefore entitled to unilateral preferences.

If we do not want to wreck this conference, we must abide strictly by principles. As an underdeveloped country we must speak about right being on our side. In our case, as a socialist country, we can also speak of the discrimination that is practiced against us not only by some developed capitalist countries but also by underdeveloped countries that, consciously or otherwise, are serving the interests of monopoly capital, which has taken over basic control of their economies.

We do not regard the existing price relationships in the world as just, as fair, but this is not the only injustice that exists. There is direct exploitation of some countries by others. There is discrimination against countries because they have different economic structures. And, as we have already pointed out, there is the invasion of foreign capital to the point where it controls a country's economy for its own ends. To be consistent, when we address requests to the developed socialist countries we should also specify what we are going to do to end discrimination, and at least to end the most obvious and dangerous forms of imperialist penetration.

We all know about the trade discrimination practiced by the imperialist countries against the socialist countries with the aim of blocking their development. At times, it has been tantamount to a real blockade, such as the almost absolute blockade maintained by United States imperialism against the German Democratic Republic, the People's Republic of China, the Democratic Republic of Korea, the Democratic Republic of Vietnam, and the Republic of Cuba. Everyone knows that this policy has failed, and that other powers that originally followed the lead of the United States have gradually parted company from it in order to secure their own profits. The failure of this policy is by now only too obvious.

Trade discrimination has also been practiced against dependent countries and socialist countries, with the ultimate aim of ensuring that the monopolies do not lose their fields of exploitation and at the same time strengthening the blockade of the socialist camp. This policy, too, is failing, and the question arises whether there is any point in remaining bound to historically doomed foreign interests, or whether the time has come to break through all the obstacles to trade and expand markets in the socialist area.

The various forms of discrimination that hamper trade, and that make it easier for the imperialists to manipulate a range of primary commodities and a number of countries producing those commodities, are still being maintained. In the nuclear age, it is simply absurd to classify products such as copper and other minerals as strategic materials and to prevent trade in them. Yet this policy has been maintained and is maintained to this day. There is also talk of so-called incompatibilities between state monopoly of foreign trade and the forms of trading adopted by the capitalist countries. Using that pretext, discriminatory relations, quotas, etc., are established—maneuvers in which GATT has played a dominant role under the official guise of combating unfair trade practices. Discrimination against state trading not only serves as a weapon against the socialist countries but is also designed to prevent the underdeveloped countries from adopting any of the most urgent measures needed to strengthen their negotiating position on the international market and to counteract the actions of the monopolies.

The suspension of economic aid by international agencies to countries adopting the socialist system of government is a further variation on the same theme. A common practice of the International Monetary Fund in recent years has been to attack bilateral payment agreements with socialist countries and to impose on its weaker members a policy of opposing this type of relations between peoples.

As we have already pointed out, all these discriminatory measures imposed by imperialism have the dual object of blockading the socialist camp and strengthening the exploitation of the underdeveloped countries.

It is undeniable that present-day prices are unfair. It is equally true that those prices are conditioned by monopoly restriction of markets and by the establishment of political relationships that make free competition a term applied one-sidedly: free competition for the monopolies—a free fox among free chickens.

Quite apart from the agreements that may emanate from this conference, opening up the large and growing markets of the socialist camp would help to raise raw material prices. The world has plenty of hunger, but not enough money to buy food. And paradoxically in the underdeveloped world, in the world of hunger, projects for increasing food production—that is, to be able to eat—are actually discouraged in order to maintain present prices. This is the inexorable law of the philosophy of plunder, which must cease to be the rule in relations between peoples.

Furthermore, it would be feasible for some underdeveloped countries to export manufactured goods to the socialist countries and even make long-term agreements so as to enable some nations to make better use of their natural wealth and specialize in certain branches of industry that would enable them to participate in world trade as producers of manufactured products. All this can be complemented by the supplying of long-term credits for the development of the industries, or branches of industry, we are considering. It must always be borne in mind, however, that certain measures with respect to relations between socialist countries and underdeveloped countries cannot be taken unilaterally.

It is a strange paradox that while in its reports the United Nations is forecasting adverse trends in the foreign trade of the underdeveloped countries, and while Dr. Prebisch, the secretary-general of the conference, is stressing the dangers that will arise if this state of affairs persists, there is still talk of the feasibility—and in some cases the necessity, as with the so-called strategic materials—of discriminating against certain states because they belong to the socialist camp.

All these anomalies are possible because of the incontrovertible fact that at the present stage of human history the underdeveloped countries are the battleground of economic systems that belong to different historical eras. In some of these countries feudalism still exists; in others a nascent, still weak bourgeoisie has to withstand the dual pressure of imperialist interests and of its own proletariat, which is fighting for a more just distribution of income. In the face of this dilemma, some national bourgeoisies have maintained their independence or adopted some forms of joint action with the proletariat, while others have made common cause with imperialism; they have become its appendages, its agents, and have transmitted this same quality to the governments representing them.

We must sound a warning that this type of dependence, skillfully used, may endanger the possibility of solid progress at the conference. But we must also point out that whatever advantages these governments may gain today, as the price of disunity, will be repaid with interest tomorrow, when in addition to facing the hostility of their own peoples they will have to stand up alone to the sudden attack of the monopolies, for whom the only law is maximum profit.

We have made a brief analysis of the causes and results of the contradictions between the socialist camp and the imperialist camp and between the camp of the exploited and that of the exploiting countries. Here are two clear dangers to world peace.

It must also be pointed out, however, that the growing boom in some capitalist countries, and their inevitable expansion in search of new markets, has led to changes in the balance of forces among them and given rise to tensions that must be taken into account if world peace is to be preserved. Do not forget that the last two world conflagrations were sparked by clashes between developed powers that could find no solution to their problems other than the use of force. We observe a series of phenomena that clearly demonstrate the growing acuteness of this struggle. This situation may involve real dangers to world peace in the future, but it is exceedingly dangerous to the smooth progress of this conference here today. There is a clear distribution of spheres of influence between the United States and other developed capitalist powers, embracing the backward continents and parts of Europe as well. If these influences are strong enough to turn the exploited countries into fields of battle for the profits of the imperialist powers, this conference will have failed.

Cuba believes, as is pointed out in the joint statement of the underdeveloped countries, that the trade problems of our countries are well known and that what is required is the adoption of clear principles and a specific action program to usher in a new era for the world. We also believe that the statement of principles submitted by the USSR and other socialist countries forms the correct basis on which to begin discussion, and we endorse it fully. Our country also supports the measures formulated at the meeting of experts at Brasilia, which would give coherent effect to the principles we advocate and will now explain.

Cuba wishes to make one point clear at the outset: we are not begging for aid. We are demanding justice; but not a justice subject to the fallacious interpretations we have so often seen prevail at international meetings. We are demanding a justice that, perhaps, the people cannot define in legal terms but for which the desire is deeply rooted in the spirit of the people, oppressed by generations of exploitation.

Cuba affirms that out of this conference should come a definition of international trade as an appropriate tool for the more rapid economic development of the underdeveloped peoples and of those subject to discrimination. This definition must provide for the elimination of all forms of discrimination and all differences, even those arising from so-called equal treatment. Treatment must be fair, and fairness, in this context, is not equality; fairness is the inequality needed to enable the exploited peoples to attain an acceptable standard of living. Our task here is to lay a foundation on which a new international division of labor can be instituted. This can be done by making full use of a country's natural resources and by steadily raising its level of production until it has achieved the most complex forms of manufacturing.

In addition, the new division of labor must be achieved by restoring to the underdeveloped countries the traditional export markets that have been seized from them by artificial measures of protectionism and subsidization of production in the developed countries, and by a fair participation in future consumption increases.

This conference should recommend specific regulations on the use of surplus primary commodities to prevent them from being turned into a form of subsidized exports of developed countries, to the detriment of the traditional exports of the underdeveloped countries, or from being turned into instruments of penetration by foreign capital of an underdeveloped country.

It is unthinkable for the underdeveloped countries to have to bear the growing burden of the foreign debt while their just demands are ignored. These countries are already sustaining huge losses from the deterioration of the terms of trade. Moreover, through the steady drain of interest payments they have already more than repaid the value of the imperialists' investments. The Cuban delegation proposes that until such time as the export prices of the underdeveloped countries reach a level sufficient to reimburse them for the losses of the past decade, all payments of dividends, interest, and principal should be suspended.

It must be made crystal clear that the domination of any country's economy by foreign capital investment, the deterioration in terms of trade, the control of one country's markets by another, discriminatory relations, and the use of force as an instrument of persuasion, are dangers to world trade and world peace.

This conference should also clearly establish the right of all nations to unrestricted freedom of trade, and the obligation of all states signing the agreement emanating from this conference to refrain from restraining trade in any manner, directly or indirectly.

The right of all countries to freely arrange the shipment of their goods by sea or air and to move them freely throughout the world without hindrance should be clearly set forth.

The conference should condemn any application or instigation of economic measures by one state to infringe the sovereign freedom of another state and to obtain from it advantages of any kind whatsoever, or to bring about the collapse of its economy. In order to achieve the foregoing, the principle of self-determination embodied in the United Nations Charter must be fully implemented. The conference should reaffirm the right of states to dispose of their own resources, to adopt the form of political and economic organization that suits them best, and to choose their own avenues of development and specialization in economic activity, without incurring reprisals of any kind whatsoever.

The conference should adopt measures for the establishment of financial, credit, and tariff organizations, with rules based on absolute equality and on justice and fairness, to replace the existing organizations, which are obsolete from the functional point of view and reprehensible from the standpoint of their specific aims.

In order to guarantee to a people the full use of its own resources, it is necessary to condemn the existence of foreign bases, the presence—temporary or otherwise—of foreign troops in a country without its consent, and the maintenance of colonial rule by some developed capitalist powers.

For all these purposes, the conference needs to reach agreement and lay a firm foundation for the establishment of an international trade organization, to be governed by the principle of the equality and universality of membership, and to possess sufficient authority to make decisions binding on all signatory states. The practice of barring from such forums countries that have won their liberation since the establishment of the United Nations, and/or that have social systems not to the liking of some of the world's powers, must be abolished.

The authority to make decisions that will be respected can come only from an organization of the kind I have described—one that will replace the existing organizations, which perpetuate the status quo and current discrimination in trade. Such authority cannot come from unenforceable formulas that lead only to endless discussions of what we already know all too well. This new type of organization is what can guarantee respect for new norms in international relations and the achievement of economic security.

Precise time periods for the establishment of each of these measures need to be set.

These are, distinguished delegates, the most important points that the Cuban delegation wished to bring to the attention of the conference. It should be pointed out that many of the ideas that are now gaining currency through being expressed by international bodies, by the precise analysis of the present situation of the developing countries submitted by Dr. Prebisch, the secretary-general of the conference, and many of the measures approved by other states—trading with socialist countries, obtaining credits from them, the need of basic social reforms for economic development, etc.—have been formulated and put into practice by Cuba during the five years of revolutionary government. Moreover, the adoption of these measures has caused our country to be subjected to unjust condemnation and to acts of economic and military aggression approved by some of the countries that now endorse those ideas.

Suffice it to recall the criticism and condemnation of Cuba for having established trade relations and cooperation with countries outside our hemisphere, and its de facto exclusion, to this day, from the Latin American regional group, organized under the auspices of the Charter of Alta Gracia, that is, of the Organization of American States, from which Cuba is excluded.[64]

We have dealt with the basic points concerning foreign trade, the need for changes in the foreign policy of the developed countries in their relations with the underdeveloped countries, and the need to restructure all international credit, financial, and similar bodies. We must emphasize, however, that these measures are not sufficient to guarantee economic development.

Other measures—which Cuba, an underdeveloped country, has put into practice—are needed as well.

As a minimum, exchange controls must be established, prohibiting remittances of funds abroad or restricting them to a significant degree; there must be state control of foreign trade; there must be agrarian reform; all natural resources must be restored to the nation; technological education must be encouraged. And other measures of internal reorganization essential to a faster rate of development must be taken.

Out of respect for the wishes of the governments represented here, Cuba has not included among the irreducible minimum measures the taking over by the state of all the means of production. But we believe that this measure would contribute to a more efficient and quicker solution to the serious problems under discussion.

And the imperialists? Will they sit with arms folded? No!

Their system is the cause of the evils from which we are suffering, but they will try to obscure the facts with twisted statements; at this they are masters. They will try to render this conference powerless and sow disunity in the camp of the exploited countries by offering them crumbs.

They will try everything to keep in place the old international bodies that serve their ends so well. They will offer reforms, but not basic ones. They will seek a way to lead the conference into a blind alley, so that it will be suspended or adjourned. They will try to rob it of importance by counterposing other meetings convened by themselves, or to see that the conference ends without achieving any tangible results.

They will not accept a new international trade organization; they will threaten to boycott it and will probably do so. They will try to show that the existing international division of labor is beneficial to all, and will refer to industrialization as a dangerous and excessive ambition.

Lastly, they will allege that the blame for underdevelopment rests with the underdeveloped. To this we can reply that to a certain extent they are right, and that they will be even more right if we show ourselves incapable of uniting, in wholehearted determination, to form a united front of victims of discrimination and exploitation.

The questions we wish to ask this assembly are these: Will we be able to carry out the task history demands of us? Will the developed capitalist countries have the political acumen to accede to the minimum demands?

If the measures stated here cannot be adopted by this conference; if all that emerges once again is a hybrid document crammed with vague statements and escape clauses; and unless, at the very least, the economic and political barriers to trade among all regions of the world and to international cooperation are removed, then the underdeveloped countries will continue to face increasingly difficult economic situations, and world tension may mount dangerously. A world conflagration may be sparked at any moment by the ambition of some imperialist country to destroy the socialist camp, or, in the not-too-distant future, by insoluble contradictions between the capitalist countries. In addition, rebelliousness will grow stronger every day among the peoples subjected to various conditions of exploitation, and they will take up arms to gain by force the rights that reason alone has not won them.

This is happening today with the peoples of so-called Portuguese Guinea and Angola, who are fighting to free themselves from the colonial yoke, and with the people of South Vietnam who, weapons in hand, stand ready to shake off the yoke of imperialism and its puppets.[65]

Let it be known that Cuba supports and applauds those peoples who, having exhausted all possibilities of a peaceful solution, have said "Enough!" to exploitation, and that their magnificent demonstration of rebellion has won our militant solidarity.

Having stated the essential points on which our analysis of the present situation is based, having put forward the recommendations we consider relevant to this conference and our views on what the future holds if no progress is made in trade relations between countries—an appropriate means of reducing tension and contributing to development—we wish to place on record our hope that the constructive discussion we spoke of will take place. The aim of our efforts is to bring about such a discussion, from which everyone will gain, and to rally the underdeveloped countries of the world to unity, so as to present a cohesive front. We place our hopes also in the success of this conference, and we join in friendship with the poor of this world and the countries in the socialist camp, putting all our powers to work for its success.

Thank you. [*Applause*]

Cuba's example shows that the peoples of the world can liberate themselves

Ernesto Che Guevara

INTRODUCTORY NOTE

On December 9, 1964, Ernesto Che Guevara left Cuba for New York, where he was scheduled to address the United Nations General Assembly as the first stop on a three-month trip that took him to eight African countries.

During Guevara's eight-day stay in New York, he met with diplomatic representatives, with Cubans living in the United States who supported the revolution, and with political activists. Among the activities he attended was a reception at the Tanzanian mission, at which he met another noted revolutionary leader—Malcolm X. He was also interviewed on the nationally televised CBS news program "Face the Nation."

As with Castro's visit four years earlier, Guevara's trip to the United States became a focus for opponents of the Cuban revolution. Anti-Cuba rallies were held outside the Cuban mission, the United Nations, and the offices of CBS. One of these was addressed by New York's governor Nelson Rockefeller.

The most serious incident occurred while Guevara was addressing the General Assembly. In the middle of his speech, a bazooka was fired at the United Nations Building from across the East River. The shell, fired from a U.S. Army–issue portable rocket launcher, fell short and landed in the water, although its explosion could be heard in the General Assembly Hall. Guevara continued his address without pause.

Ernesto Che Guevara

Cuba's example shows that the peoples of the world can liberate themselves

Address to General Assembly
December 11, 1964

Mr. President;
Distinguished delegates:

The Delegation of Cuba to this assembly, first of all, is pleased to fulfill the agreeable duty of welcoming the addition of three new nations to the important number of those that discuss the problems of the world here. We therefore greet, in the persons of their presidents and prime ministers, the peoples of Zambia, Malawi, and Malta, and express the hope that from the outset these countries will be added to the group of Non-aligned countries that struggle against imperialism, colonialism, and neocolonialism.

We also wish to convey our congratulations to the president of this assembly [Alex Quaison-Sackey of Ghana], whose elevation to so high a post is of special significance since it reflects this new historic stage of resounding triumphs for the peoples of Africa, who up until recently were subject to the colonial system of imperialism. Today, in their immense majority these peoples have become sovereign states through the legitimate exercise of their self-determination. The final hour of colonialism has struck, and millions of inhabitants of Africa, Asia, and Latin America rise to meet a new life and demand their unrestricted right to self-determination and to the independent development of their nations.

We wish you, Mr. President, the greatest success in the tasks entrusted to you by the member states.

Cuba comes here to state its position on the most important points of controversy and will do so with the full sense of responsibility that the use of this rostrum implies, while at the same time fulfilling the unavoidable duty of speaking clearly and frankly.

We would like to see this assembly shake itself out of complacency and move forward. We would like to see the committees begin their work and not stop at the first confrontation. Imperialism wants to turn this meeting into a pointless oratorical tournament, instead of solving the serious problems of the world. We must prevent it from doing so. This session of the assembly should not be remembered in the future solely by the number nineteen that identifies it. Our efforts are directed to that end.

We feel that we have the right and the obligation to do so, because our country is one of the most constant points of friction. It is one of the places where the principles upholding the right of small countries to sovereignty are put to the test day by day, minute by minute. At the same time our country is one of the trenches of freedom in the world, situated a few steps away from United States imperialism, showing by its actions, its daily example, that in the present conditions of humanity the peoples can liberate themselves and can keep themselves free.

Of course, there now exists a socialist camp that becomes stronger day by day and has more powerful weapons of struggle. But additional conditions are required for survival: the maintenance of internal unity, faith in one's own destiny, and the irrevocable decision to fight to the death for the defense of one's country and revolution. These conditions, distinguished delegates, exist in Cuba.

Of all the burning problems to be dealt with by this assembly, one of special significance for us, and one whose solution we feel must be found first—so as to leave no doubt in the minds of anyone—is that of peaceful coexistence among states with different economic and social systems. Much progress has been made in the world in this field. But imperialism, particularly U.S. imperialism, has attempted to make the world believe that peaceful coexistence is the exclusive right of the earth's great powers. We say here what our president said in Cairo, and what later was expressed in the declaration of the Second Conference of Heads of State or Government of Nonaligned Countries: that peaceful coexistence cannot be limited to the powerful countries if we want to ensure world peace.[66] Peaceful coexistence must be exercised among all states, regardless of size, regardless of the previous historical relations that linked them, and regardless of the problems that may arise among some of them at a given moment.

At present, the type of peaceful coexistence to which we aspire is often violated. Merely because the Kingdom of Cambodia maintained a neutral attitude and did not bow to the machinations of United States imperialism, it has been subjected to all kinds of treacherous and brutal attacks from the Yankee bases in South Vietnam.

Laos, a divided country, has also been the object of imperialist aggression of every kind. Its people have been massacred from the air. The conventions concluded at Geneva have been violated, and part of its territory is in constant danger of cowardly attacks by imperialist forces.[67]

The Democratic Republic of Vietnam knows all these histories of aggression as do few nations on earth. It has once again seen its frontier violated, has seen enemy bombers and fighter planes attack its installations, and has seen U.S. warships, violating territorial waters, attack its naval posts. At this time, the threat hangs over the Democratic Republic of Vietnam that the U.S. war makers may openly extend into its territory the war that for many years they have been waging against the people of South Vietnam. The Soviet Union and the People's Republic of China have given serious warnings to the United States. We are faced with a case in which world peace is in danger and, moreover, the lives of millions of human beings in this part of Asia are constantly threatened and subjected to the whim of the U.S. invader.

Peaceful coexistence has also been brutally put to the test in Cyprus, due to pressures from the Turkish government and NATO, compelling the people and the government of Cyprus to make a heroic and firm stand in defense of their sovereignty.[68]

In all these parts of the world, imperialism attempts to impose its version of what coexistence should be. It is the oppressed peoples in alliance with the socialist camp that must show them what true coexistence is, and it is the obligation of the United Nations to support them.

We must also state that it is not only in relations among sovereign states that the concept of peaceful coexistence needs to be precisely defined. As Marxists we have maintained that peaceful coexistence among nations does not encompass coexistence between the exploiters and the exploited, between the oppressors and the oppressed. Furthermore, the right to full independence from all forms of colonial oppression is a fundamental principle of this organization. That is why we express our solidarity with the colonial peoples of so-called Portuguese Guinea, Angola, and Mozambique, who have been massacred for the crime of demanding their freedom.[69] And we are prepared to help them to the extent of our ability in accordance with the Cairo declaration.

We express our solidarity with the people of Puerto Rico and their great leader, Pedro Albizu Campos, who, in another act of hypocrisy, has been set free at the age of seventy-two, almost unable to speak, paralyzed, after spending a lifetime in jail. Albizu Campos is a symbol of the as yet unfree but indomitable Latin America. Years and years of prison, almost unbearable pressures in jail, mental torture, solitude, total isolation from his people and his family, the insolence of the conqueror and its lackeys in the land of his birth—nothing broke his will. The delegation of Cuba, on behalf of its people, pays a tribute of admiration and gratitude to a patriot who confers honor upon Our America.[70]

The United States for many years has tried to convert Puerto Rico into a model of hybrid culture: the Spanish language with English inflections, the Spanish language with hinges on its backbone—the better to bow down before the Yankee soldier. Puerto Rican soldiers have been used as cannon fodder in imperialist wars, as in Korea, and have even been made to fire at their own brothers, as in the massacre perpetrated by the U.S. army a few months ago against the unarmed people of Panama—one of the most recent crimes carried out by Yankee imperialism.[71] And yet, despite this assault on their will and their historical destiny, the people of Puerto Rico have preserved their culture, their Latin character, their national feelings, which in themselves give proof of the implacable desire for independence lying within the masses of that Latin American island.

We must also warn that the principle of peaceful coexistence does not encompass the right to mock the will of the peoples, as is happening in the case of so-called British Guiana. There the government of Prime Minister Cheddi Jagan has been the victim of every kind of pressure and maneuver, and independence has been delayed to gain time to find ways to flout the people's will and guarantee the docility of a new government, placed in power by covert means, in order to grant a castrated freedom to this country of the Americas.[72] Whatever roads Guiana may be compelled to follow to obtain independence, the moral and militant support of Cuba goes to its people.

Furthermore, we must point out that the islands of Guadaloupe and Martinique have been fighting for a long time for self-government without obtaining it. This state of affairs must not continue.

Once again we speak out to put the world on guard against what is happening in South Africa. The brutal policy of apartheid is applied before the eyes of the nations of the world. The peoples of Africa are compelled to endure the fact that on the African continent the superiority of one race over another remains official policy, and that in the name of this racial superiority murder is committed with impunity. Can the United Nations do nothing to stop this?

I would like to refer specifically to the painful case of the Congo, unique in the history of the modern world, which shows how, with absolute impunity, with the most insolent cynicism, the rights of peoples can be flouted. The direct reason for all this is the enormous wealth of the Congo, which the imperialist countries want to keep under their control. In the speech he made during his first visit to the United Nations, Compañero Fidel Castro observed that the whole problem of coexistence among peoples boils down to the wrongful appropriation of other peoples' wealth. He made the following statement: "End the philosophy of plunder and the philosophy of war will be ended as well."

But the philosophy of plunder has not only not been ended, it is stronger than ever. And that is why those who used the name of the United Nations to commit the murder of Lumumba are today, in the name of the defense of the white race, murdering thousands of Congolese. How can we forget the betrayal of the hope that Patrice Lumumba placed in the United Nations? How can we forget the machinations and maneuvers that followed in the wake of the occupation of that country by United Nations troops, under whose auspices the assassins of this great African patriot acted with impunity? How can we forget, distinguished delegates, that the one who flouted the authority of the UN in the Congo—and not exactly for patriotic reasons, but rather by virtue of conflicts between imperialists—was Moise Tshombe, who initiated the secession of Katanga with

Belgian support? And how can one justify, how can one explain, that at the end of all the United Nations activities there, Tshombe, dislodged from Katanga, should return as lord and master of the Congo?[73] Who can deny the sad role that the imperialists compelled the United Nations to play?

To sum up: dramatic mobilizations were carried out to avoid the secession of Katanga, but today Tshombe is in power, the wealth of the Congo is in imperialist hands—and the expenses have to be paid by the honorable nations. The merchants of war certainly do good business! That is why the government of Cuba supports the just stance of the Soviet Union in refusing to pay the expenses for this crime.

And as if this were not enough, we now have flung in our faces these latest acts that have filled the world with indignation.[74] Who are the perpetrators? Belgian paratroopers, carried by United States planes, who took off from British bases. We remember as if it were yesterday that we saw a small country in Europe, a civilized and industrious country, the Kingdom of Belgium, invaded by Hitler's hordes. We were embittered by the knowledge that this small nation was massacred by German imperialism, and we felt affection for its people. But this other side of the imperialist coin was the one that many of us did not see. Perhaps the sons of Belgian patriots who died defending their country's liberty are now murdering in cold blood thousands of Congolese in the name of the white race, just as they suffered under the German heel because their blood was not sufficiently Aryan.

Our free eyes open now on new horizons and can see what yesterday, in our condition as colonial slaves, we could not observe: that "Western civilization" disguises behind its showy facade a picture of hyenas and jackals. That is the only name that can be applied to those who have gone to fulfill such "humanitarian" tasks in the Congo. A carnivorous animal that feeds on unarmed peoples. That is what imperialism does to men. That is what distinguishes the imperial "white man."

All free men of the world must be prepared to avenge the

crime of the Congo.[75] Perhaps many of those soldiers, who were turned into subhumans by imperialist machinery, believe in good faith that they are defending the rights of a superior race. In this assembly, however, those peoples whose skins are darkened by a different sun, colored by different pigments, constitute the majority. And they fully and clearly understand that the difference between men does not lie in the color of their skin, but in the forms of ownership of the means of production, in the relations of production.

The Cuban delegation extends greetings to the peoples of Southern Rhodesia and South-West Africa, oppressed by white colonialist minorities; to the peoples of Basutoland, Bechuanaland, Swaziland, French Somaliland, the Arabs of Palestine, Aden and the Protectorates, Oman; and to all peoples in conflict with imperialism and colonialism. We reaffirm our support to them.[76]

I express also the hope that there will be a just solution to the conflict facing our sister republic of Indonesia in its relations with Malaysia.[77]

Mr. President: One of the fundamental themes of this conference is general and complete disarmament. We express our support for general and complete disarmament. Furthermore, we advocate the complete destruction of all thermonuclear devices and we support the holding of a conference of all the nations of the world to make this aspiration of all people a reality. In his statement before this assembly, our prime minister warned that arms races have always led to war. There are new nuclear powers in the world, and the possibilities of a confrontation are growing.

We believe that such a conference is necessary to obtain the total destruction of thermonuclear weapons and, as a first step, the total prohibition of tests. At the same time, we have to establish clearly the duty of all countries to respect the present borders of other states and to refrain from engaging in any aggression, even with conventional weapons.

In adding our voice to that of all the peoples of the world

who ask for general and complete disarmament, the destruction of all nuclear arsenals, the complete halt to the building of new thermonuclear devices and of nuclear tests of any kind, we believe it necessary to also stress that the territorial integrity of nations must be respected and the armed hand of imperialism held back, for it is no less dangerous when it uses only conventional weapons. Those who murdered thousands of defenseless citizens of the Congo did not use the atomic bomb. They used conventional weapons. Conventional weapons have also been used by imperialism, causing so many deaths.

Even if the measures advocated here were to become effective and make it unnecessary to mention it, we must point out that we cannot adhere to any regional pact for denuclearization so long as the United States maintains aggressive bases on our own territory, in Puerto Rico, Panama, and in other Latin American states where it feels it has the right to place both conventional and nuclear weapons without any restrictions. We feel that we must be able to provide for our own defense in the light of the recent resolution of the Organization of American States against Cuba, on the basis of which an attack may be carried out invoking the Rio Treaty.[78]

If the conference to which we have just referred were to achieve all these objectives—which, unfortunately, would be difficult—we believe it would be the most important one in the history of humanity. To ensure this it would be necessary for the People's Republic of China to be represented, and that is why a conference of this type must be held. But it would be much simpler for the peoples of the world to recognize the undeniable truth of the existence of the People's Republic of China, whose government is the sole representative of its people, and to give it the seat it deserves, which is, at present, usurped by the gang that controls the province of Taiwan, with United States support.

The problem of the representation of China in the United Nations cannot in any way be considered as a case of a new admission to the organization, but rather as the restoration of the legitimate rights of the People's Republic of China.

We must repudiate energetically the "two Chinas" plot. The Chiang Kai-shek gang of Taiwan cannot remain in the United Nations. What we are dealing with, we repeat, is the expulsion of the usurper and the installation of the legitimate representative of the Chinese people.[79]

We also warn against the United States government's insistence on presenting the problem of the legitimate representation of China in the UN as an "important question," in order to impose a requirement of a two-thirds majority of members present and voting. The admission of the People's Republic of China to the United Nations is, in fact, an important question for the entire world, but not for the machinery of the United Nations, where it must constitute a mere question of procedure. In this way justice will be done. Almost as important as attaining justice, however, would be the demonstration, once and for all, that this august assembly has eyes to see, ears to hear, tongues to speak with, and sound criteria for making its decisions.

The proliferation of nuclear weapons among the member states of NATO, and especially the possession of these devices of mass destruction by the Federal Republic of Germany, would make the possibility of an agreement on disarmament even more remote, and linked to such an agreement is the problem of the peaceful reunification of Germany. So long as there is no clear understanding, the existence of two Germanys must be recognized: that of the German Democratic Republic and the Federal Republic. The German problem can be solved only with the direct participation in negotiations of the German Democratic Republic with full rights.[80]

We shall only touch on the questions of economic development and international trade that are broadly represented in the agenda. In this very year of 1964 the Geneva conference was held at which a multitude of matters related to these aspects of international relations were dealt with. The warnings and forecasts of our delegation were fully confirmed, to the misfortune of the economically dependent countries.

We wish only to point out that insofar as Cuba is concerned, the United States of America has not implemented the explicit recommendations of that conference,[81] and recently the U.S. government also prohibited the sale of medicines to Cuba. By doing so it divested itself, once and for all, of the mask of humanitarianism with which it attempted to disguise the aggressive nature of its blockade against the people of Cuba.

Furthermore, we state once more that the scars left by colonialism that impede the development of the peoples are expressed not only in political relations. The so-called deterioration of the terms of trade is nothing but the result of the unequal exchange between countries producing raw materials and industrial countries, which dominate markets and impose the illusory justice of equal exchange of values.

So long as the economically dependent peoples do not free themselves from the capitalist markets and, in a firm bloc with the socialist countries, impose new relations between the exploited and the exploiters, there will be no solid economic development. In certain cases there will be retrogression, in which the weak countries will fall under the political domination of the imperialists and colonialists.

Finally, distinguished delegates, it must be made clear that in the area of the Caribbean, maneuvers and preparations for aggression against Cuba are taking place, on the coasts of Nicaragua above all, in Costa Rica as well, in the Panama Canal Zone, on Vieques Island in Puerto Rico, in Florida, and possibly in other parts of United States territory and perhaps also in Honduras. In these places Cuban mercenaries are training, as well as mercenaries of other nationalities, with a purpose that cannot be the most peaceful one.

After a big scandal, the government of Costa Rica—it is said—has ordered the elimination of all training camps of Cuban exiles in that country. No one knows whether this position is sincere, or whether it is simply an alibi because the mercenaries training there were about to commit some misdeed. We hope that full cognizance will be taken of the real existence of bases for aggression, which we denounced long ago, and that the world will ponder the international responsibility of the government of a country that authorizes and facilitates the training of mercenaries to attack Cuba.

We should note that news of the training of mercenaries in different parts of the Caribbean and the participation of the U.S. government in such acts is presented as completely natural in the newspapers in the United States. We know of no Latin American voice that has officially protested this. This shows the cynicism with which the United States government moves its pawns.

The sharp foreign ministers of the OAS had eyes to see Cuban emblems and to find "irrefutable" proof in the weapons that the Yankees exhibited in Venezuela, but they do not see the preparations for aggression in the United States, just as they did not hear the voice of President Kennedy, who explicitly declared himself the aggressor against Cuba at Playa Girón. In some cases, it is a blindness provoked by the hatred against our revolution by the ruling classes of the Latin American countries. In others—and these are sadder and more deplorable—it is the product of the dazzling glitter of mammon.

As is well known, after the tremendous commotion of the so-called Caribbean crisis, the United States undertook certain commitments with the Soviet Union. These culminated in the withdrawal of certain types of weapons that the continued acts of aggression of the United States—such as the mercenary attack at Playa Girón and threats of invasion against our homeland—had compelled us to install in Cuba as an act of legitimate and essential defense.

The United States, furthermore, tried to get the UN to inspect our territory. But we emphatically refuse, since Cuba does not recognize the right of the United States, or of anyone else in the world, to determine the type of weapons Cuba may have within its borders.

In this connection, we would abide only by multilateral

agreements, with equal obligations for all the parties concerned. As Fidel Castro has said:

> So long as the concept of sovereignty exists as the pre-rogative of nations and of independent peoples, as a right of all peoples, we will not accept the exclusion of our people from that right. So long as the world is governed by these principles, so long as the world is governed by those concepts that have universal validity because they are universally accepted and recognized by the peoples, we will not accept the attempt to deprive us of any of those rights, and we will renounce none of those rights.

The secretary-general of the United Nations, U Thant, understood our reasons. Nevertheless, the United States attempted to establish a new prerogative, an arbitrary and illegal one: that of violating the airspace of a small country. Thus, we see flying over our country U-2 aircraft and other types of spy planes that, with complete impunity, fly over our airspace. We have made all the necessary warnings for the violations of our airspace to cease, as well as for a halt to the provocations of the United States Navy against our sentry posts in the zone of Guantánamo, the buzzing by aircraft of our ships or the ships of other nationalities in international waters, the pirate attacks against ships sailing under different flags, and the infiltration of spies, saboteurs, and weapons onto our island.

We want to build socialism. We have declared that we are supporters of those who strive for peace. We have declared ourselves to be within the group of Nonaligned countries, although we are Marxist-Leninists, because the Nonaligned countries, like ourselves, fight imperialism. We want peace. We want to build a better life for our people. That is why we avoid, insofar as possible, falling into the provocations manufactured by the Yankees. But we know the mentality of those who govern them. They want to make us pay a very high price for that peace. We reply that the price cannot go beyond the bounds of dignity.

And Cuba reaffirms once again the right to maintain on its territory the weapons it deems appropriate, and its refusal to recognize the right of any power on earth—no matter how powerful—to violate our soil, our territorial waters, or our airspace.

If in any assembly Cuba assumes obligations of a collective nature, it will fulfill them to the letter. So long as this does not happen, Cuba maintains all its rights, just as any other nation. In the face of the demands of imperialism, our prime minister laid out the five points necessary for the existence of a secure peace in the Caribbean.

They are:

1. A halt to the economic blockade and all economic and trade pressures by the United States, in all parts of the world, against our country.

2. A halt to all subversive activities, launching and landing of weapons and explosives by air and sea, organization of mercenary invasions, infiltration of spies and saboteurs, acts all carried out from the territory of the United States and some accomplice countries.

3. A halt to pirate attacks carried out from existing bases in the United States and Puerto Rico.

4. A halt to all the violations of our airspace and our territorial waters by United States aircraft and warships.

5. Withdrawal from the Guantánamo naval base and return of the Cuban territory occupied by the United States.[82]

None of these elementary demands has been met, and our forces are still being provoked from the naval base at Guantánamo. That base has become a nest of thieves and a launching pad for them into our territory. We would tire this assembly were we to give a detailed account of the large number of provocations of all kinds. Suffice it to say that including the first days of December the number amounts to 1,323 in 1964 alone. The list covers minor provocations such as violation of the boundary line, launching of objects from the territory controlled by the United States, the commission of acts of sexual exhibitionism by U.S. personnel of both sexes, and verbal insults. It includes others that are more serious, such as shooting off small-caliber weapons, aiming weapons at our territory, and offenses against our national flag. Extremely serious provocations include those of crossing the boundary line and starting fires in installations on the Cuban side, as well as rifle fire. There have been seventy-eight rifle shots this year, with the sorrowful toll of one death: that of Ramón López Peña, a soldier, killed by two shots fired from the United States post three and a half kilometers from the coast on the northern boundary. This extremely grave provocation took place at 7:07 p.m. on July 19, 1964, and the prime minister of our government publicly stated on July 26 that if the event were to recur he would give orders for our troops to repel the aggression. At the same time orders were given for the withdrawal of the forward line of Cuban forces to positions farther away from the boundary line and construction of the necessary fortified positions.

One thousand three hundred and twenty-three provocations in 340 days amount to approximately four per day. Only a perfectly disciplined army with a morale such as ours could resist so many hostile acts without losing its self-control.

Forty-seven countries meeting at the Second Conference of Heads of State or Government of Nonaligned Countries in Cairo unanimously agreed:

> Noting with concern that foreign military bases are in practice a means of bringing pressure on nations and retarding their emancipation and development, based on their own ideological, political, economic, and cultural ideas, the conference declares its full support to the countries which are seeking to secure the evacuation of foreign bases on their territory and calls upon all states maintaining troops and bases in other countries to remove them forthwith.

> The conference considers that the maintenance at Guantánamo (Cuba) of a military base of the United States of America, in defiance of the will of the government and people of Cuba and in defiance of the provisions embodied in the

declaration of the Belgrade conference, constitutes a violation of Cuba's sovereignty and territorial integrity.

Noting that the Cuban government expresses its readiness to settle its dispute over the base of Guantánamo with the United States of America on an equal footing, the conference urges the United States government to negotiate the evacuation of this base with the Cuban government.

The government of the United States has not responded to this request of the Cairo conference and is attempting to maintain indefinitely by force its occupation of a piece of our territory, from which it carries out acts of aggression such as those detailed earlier.

The Organization of American States—which the people also call the United States Ministry of Colonies—condemned us "energetically," even though it had just excluded us from its midst, ordering its members to break off diplomatic and trade relations with Cuba. The OAS authorized aggression against our country at any time and under any pretext, violating the most fundamental international laws, completely disregarding the United Nations. Uruguay, Bolivia, Chile, and Mexico opposed that measure, and the government of the United States of Mexico refused to comply with the sanctions that had been approved. Since then we have had no relations with any Latin American countries except Mexico, and this fulfills one of the necessary conditions for direct aggression by imperialism.

We want to make clear once again that our concern for Latin America is based on the ties that unite us: the language we speak, the culture we maintain, and the common master we had. We have no other reason for desiring the liberation of Latin America from the U.S. colonial yoke. If any of the Latin American countries here decide to reestablish relations with Cuba, we would be willing to do so on the basis of equality, and without viewing that recognition of Cuba as a free country in the world to be a gift to our government. Because we won that recognition with our blood in the days of the liberation struggle.

We acquired it with our blood in the defense of our shores against the Yankee invasion.

Although we reject any accusations against us of interference in the internal affairs of other countries, we cannot deny that we sympathize with those people who strive for their freedom. We must fulfill the obligation of our government and people to state clearly and categorically to the world that we morally support and stand in solidarity with peoples who struggle anywhere in the world to make a reality of the rights of full sovereignty proclaimed in the United Nations Charter.

It is the United States that intervenes. It has done so historically in Latin America. Since the end of the last century Cuba has experienced this truth; but it has been experienced, too, by Venezuela, Nicaragua, Central America in general, Mexico, Haiti, and the Dominican Republic. In recent years, apart from our people, Panama has experienced direct aggression, where the marines in the Canal Zone opened fire in cold blood against the defenseless people; the Dominican Republic, whose coast was violated by the Yankee fleet to avoid an outbreak of the just fury of the people after the death of Trujillo; and Colombia, whose capital was taken by assault as a result of a rebellion provoked by the assassination of Gaitán.[83]

Covert interventions are carried out through military missions that participate in internal repression, organizing forces designed for that purpose in many countries, and also in coups d'état, which have been repeated so frequently on the Latin American continent during recent years. Concretely, United States forces intervened in the repression of the peoples of Venezuela, Colombia, and Guatemala, who fought with weapons for their freedom. In Venezuela, not only do U.S. forces advise the army and the police, but they also direct acts of genocide carried out from the air against the peasant population in vast insurgent areas. And the Yankee companies operating there exert pressures of every kind to increase direct interference. The imperialists are preparing to repress the peoples of the Americas and are establishing an International of Crime.

The United States intervenes in Latin America invoking the defense of free institutions. The time will come when this assembly will acquire greater maturity and demand of the United States government guarantees for the lives of the Blacks and Latin Americans who live in that country, most of them U.S. citizens by origin or adoption.

Those who kill their own children and discriminate daily against them because of the color of their skin; those who let the murderers of Blacks remain free, protecting them, and furthermore punishing the Black population because they demand their legitimate rights as free men—how can those who do this consider themselves guardians of freedom? We understand that today the assembly is not in a position to ask for explanations of these acts. It must be clearly established, however, that the government of the United States is not the champion of freedom, but rather the perpetuator of exploitation and oppression against the peoples of the world and against a large part of its own population.

To the ambiguous language with which some delegates have described the case of Cuba and the OAS, we reply with clear-cut words and we proclaim that the peoples of Latin America will make those servile, sell-out governments pay for their treason.

Cuba, distinguished delegates, a free and sovereign state with no chains binding it to anyone, with no foreign investments on its territory, with no proconsuls directing its policy, can speak with its head held high in this assembly and can demonstrate the justice of the phrase by which it has been baptized: "Free Territory of the Americas."

Our example will bear fruit in the continent, as it is already doing to a certain extent in Guatemala, Colombia, and Venezuela.

There is no small enemy nor insignificant force, because no longer are there isolated peoples. As the Second Declaration of Havana states:

No nation in Latin America is weak—because each forms part of a family of 200 million brothers, who suffer the same miseries, who harbor the same sentiments, who have the same enemy, who dream about the same better future, and who count upon the solidarity of all honest men and women throughout the world. . . .

This epic before us is going to be written by the hungry Indian masses, the peasants without land, the exploited workers. It is going to be written by the progressive masses, the honest and brilliant intellectuals, who so greatly abound in our suffering Latin American lands. A struggle of masses and of ideas. An epic that will be carried forward by our peoples, mistreated and scorned by imperialism; our people, unreckoned with until today, who are now beginning to shake off their slumber. Imperialism considered us a weak and submissive flock; and now it begins to be terrified of that flock; a gigantic flock of 200 million Latin Americans in whom Yankee monopoly capitalism now sees its gravediggers. . . .

But now from one end of the continent to the other they are signaling with clarity that the hour has come—the hour of their vindication. Now this anonymous mass, this America of color, somber, taciturn America, which all over the continent sings with the same sadness and disillusionment, now this mass is beginning to enter definitively into its own history, is beginning to write it with its own blood, is beginning to suffer and die for it.

Because now in the mountains and fields of America, on its flatlands and in its jungles, in the wilderness or in the traffic of cities, on the banks of its great oceans or rivers, this world is beginning to tremble. Anxious hands are stretched forth, ready to die for what is theirs, to win those rights that were laughed at by one and all for five hundred years. Yes, now history will have to take the poor of America into account, the exploited and spurned of America, who have decided to begin writing their history for themselves for all time. Already they can be seen on the roads, on foot, day after day, in an endless march of hundreds of kilometers to the governmental "eminences," there to obtain their rights.

Already they can be seen armed with stones, sticks, machetes, in one direction and another, each day, occupying lands, sinking hooks into the land that belongs to them and defending it with their lives. They can be seen carrying signs, slogans, flags; letting them flap in the mountain or prairie winds. And the wave of anger, of demands for justice, of claims for rights trampled underfoot, which is beginning to sweep the lands of Latin America, will not stop. That wave will swell with every passing day. For that wave is composed of the greatest number, the majorities in every respect, those whose labor amasses the wealth and turns the wheels of history. Now they are awakening from the long, brutalizing sleep to which they had been subjected.

For this great mass of humanity has said, "Enough!" and has begun to march. And their march of giants will not be halted until they conquer true independence—for which they have vainly died more than once. Today, however, those who die will die like the Cubans at Playa Girón. They will die for their own true and never-to-be-surrendered independence.

All this, distinguished delegates, this new will of a whole continent, of Latin America, is made manifest in the cry proclaimed daily by our masses as the irrefutable expression of their decision to fight and to paralyze the armed hand of the invader. It is a cry that has the understanding and support of all the peoples of the world and especially of the socialist camp, headed by the Soviet Union.

That cry is: Patria o muerte! [Homeland or death]

Cuba will continue to call things by their right names

Ernesto Che Guevara

INTRODUCTORY NOTE

After Guevara's address to the General Assembly, representatives from the governments of Costa Rica, Nicaragua, Panama, Venezuela, and Colombia, took the floor to reply to his remarks, as did U.S. representative Adlai Stevenson. The following speech was Guevara's rejoinder.

Ernesto Che Guevara

Cuba will continue to call things by their right names

Reply to General Assembly debate
December 11, 1964

I wish to apologize for having to speak a second time from this rostrum. I do so in exercise of my right of reply. Of course, this could be called a counter-reply, and we could go on and on in this fashion, having counter-replies to counter-replies ad infinitum.

We shall reply one by one to the statements of those representatives who criticized Cuba's address, and we shall do so more or less in the spirit in which each of them spoke.

I shall begin by replying to the representative of Costa Rica, who regretted that Cuba had allowed itself to be influenced by certain false information appearing in the yellow press. He stated that his government had taken immediate investigative measures after the "free press" of Costa Rica—which is quite different from the "slave press" of Cuba—printed some accusations.[84]

Perhaps the representative of Costa Rica is right. We cannot make a definitive statement based on reports appearing in the imperialist press—especially that of the United States—concerning the Cuban counterrevolutionaries. But if Artime was the head of the failed invasion at Playa Girón,[85] this was done by him through an intermediary, since he returned to the United States as soon as they landed on Cuban shores and suffered the first casualties. And this intermediary, like the majority of the members of that "heroic liberation expedition" must have been a "cook" or a "dishwasher"—since this is what all these "liberators of Cuba" claimed to be after they were taken prisoner.

Artime, who has again become the chief, was indignant at the accusation that they are smugglers of whiskey. According to him they do not smuggle whiskey at their bases in Costa Rica and Nicaragua, they are only "training revolutionaries to liberate Cuba." These statements were made to the news agencies and have been published around the world.

The existence of these counterrevolutionaries has been repeatedly denounced in Costa Rica. Costa Rican patriots have informed us of the existence of these bases in the Tortugueras zone and in neighboring regions, and the government of Costa Rica must know very well whether these reports are true or not. We are absolutely convinced they are true. We are equally convinced that among his many "revolutionary activities," Mr. Artime has also found time to smuggle some whiskey, since this is natural among the type of "liberators" that the government of Costa Rica protects, even if only partially.

We have maintained over and over again that revolutions are not exportable. Revolutions are born among the people themselves. Revolutions are engendered by the exploitation of the people carried out by governments such as those of Costa Rica, Nicaragua, Panama, and Venezuela. Later on, assistance can be given or not given to liberation movements; above all they can be supported morally. But the reality is that revolutions cannot be exported.

We say this not by way of justification before this assembly; it is simply a well-known scientific fact. Therefore, it would be foolish for us to try to export revolutions—much less to Costa Rica, where, speaking truthfully, there is a regime with which we have no communication of any kind, and which is not one of those regimes in Latin America most noted for direct and indiscriminate oppression of its people.

With regard to Nicaragua, I would like to respond to its representative, although I did not quite understand his point about accents—I think he referred to Cuba, Argentina, and perhaps to the Soviet Union as well.[86] In any case, I hope the Nicaraguan representative did not detect a U.S. accent in my speech, because that would be dangerous. It may well be that I have a trace of an Argentine accent; after all, I was born there and it is no secret to anyone. I am both a Cuban and an Argentine.

I will also say something more that I hope does not offend the very illustrious representatives of Latin America seated here: I am a patriot of Latin America and of all Latin American countries. Whenever necessary I would be ready to lay down my life for the liberation of any Latin American country, without asking anything from anyone, without demanding anything, without exploiting anyone. And this is not just the frame of mind of the individual addressing this assembly at present; it is the frame of mind of the entire Cuban people. The entire Cuban people feel it whenever an injustice is committed not only in Latin America but anywhere in the world. We can quote the marvelous words of Martí that we often repeat: "Every true man must feel on his own cheek every blow struck against the cheek of another."[87] That, distinguished representatives, is the feeling of all the people of Cuba.

If the representative of Nicaragua wishes to find on a map or inspect difficult-to-reach places, he could go to Puerto Cabezas. I do not think he will deny that this was the spot where most of the Playa Girón expedition left from. He could also go to Bluefields or Monkey Point—in Spanish I believe it would be called "Punto Mono"; I don't know by what strange historical accident this place in Nicaragua is named Monkey Point rather than Punto Mono. There he would find some counterrevolutionary Cubans, or "Cuban revolutionaries"—as the representative of Nicaragua prefers to call them—of all types. There is also a good deal of whiskey there; I don't know whether it's smuggled or imported. We are aware of those bases. Naturally, we are not going to demand an OAS investigation to determine whether they are there or not. We know the collective blindness of the OAS too well to make such an absurd request.

It has been said that we have admitted having atomic weapons. We have none. I think the representative of Nicaragua made a slight mistake. We have simply defended our right to have whatever weapons we are able to acquire for our defense. And we have denied the right of any country to determine what type of weapons we should have.

The representative of Panama, who was kind enough to refer to me as Che—the name given me by the Cuban people—began by speaking about the Mexican revolution. The Cuban representative had spoken of the U.S. massacre of the people of Panama, and the Panamanian representative began by speaking about the Mexican revolution. And he continued along these lines without referring at all to the U.S. massacre, as a result of which the Panamanian government broke relations with the United States. Perhaps in the parlance of sell-out politics this might be called a tactic. But in revolutionary parlance, gentlemen, this is called abject behavior in every sense of the term.

The representative of Panama referred to the invasion in 1959. A group of adventurers led by a coffeehouse *barbudo*—who had never been in the Sierra Maestra mountains, and who is now in Miami or some other counterrevolutionary base—were stirred up to embark upon that adventure.[88] Officials of the Cuban government worked together with the government of Panama to liquidate that undertaking. It is true that they left from a Cuban port, but it is also true that we discussed the matter in a friendly manner with the Panamanian government at the time.

Of all the speeches made here against the Cuban delegation, the most inexcusable in every sense was the one by the representative of Panama. We had not the slightest intention of offending him or his government. But at the same time we had not the slightest intention of defending the Panamanian government. Our goal was to defend the Panamanian people by denouncing the U.S. massacre before the United Nations, since the Panamanian government has neither the courage nor the dignity to call things here by their right names. Our intention was neither to offend nor defend the Panamanian government. Our sympathy goes to the sister people of Panama, and we tried to defend them through our denunciation.

Among the assertions made by the representative of Panama was a most interesting one. He said that in spite of Cuban boasts, the Guantánamo base is still there. In our address, which is still fresh in the minds of the delegates, it will be recalled that we denounced the more than 11,300 provocations at the base, from the most insignificant to the firing of shots. We explained how we do not want to be provoked, because we know what the consequences could be for our people. We have brought up the problem of the Guantánamo base at every international conference, and have always asserted the right of the Cuban people to recover this base by peaceful means.

We have never engaged in boasting. The reason for this is that men such as us who are ready to die and who lead an entire people ready to die to defend their cause have no need of boasting. We did not boast at Playa Girón. We did not boast during the October crisis, when all our people faced the danger of an atomic mushroom cloud, with which the United States threatened us. At the time, all our people marched off to the trenches, or to the factories to increase production. No one retreated or complained. Thousands upon thousands of men who had not previously belonged to our militia volunteered to join, at a time when U.S. imperialism was threatening to launch a nuclear attack on Cuba. That is our country! Such a country, whose leaders and people we can proudly say have not the slightest fear of death, and who take full responsibility for their acts, never engages in boasting. To fight to the death, yes, if necessary. We can say to the distinguished representative of Panama that all the people of Cuba, together with their government, will fight to the death if we are attacked.

The representative of Colombia, speaking in a very measured tone—which I shall also use—stated that two incorrect assertions had been made. The first concerned the U.S. invasion of 1948 following the assassination of Jorge Eliecer Gaitán. From the tone of voice used by the representative of Colombia, it is clear that he was deeply affected by that death. What we referred to in our speech was a previous intervention that the representative of Colombia has perhaps forgotten: the U.S. intervention surrounding the secession of Panama.[89]

The representative of Colombia then stated that there were no liberation forces in Colombia because there was nothing to liberate. In Colombia, they speak so naturally of representative democracy. They have only two political parties there, which for years have divided up the power between them—fifty-fifty—in accordance with some fantastic kind of democracy. The Colombian oligarchy, one could say, has reached the very pinnacle of democracy. It is divided into Liberals and Conservatives, Conservatives and Liberals; four years for one, four years for the other. Nothing changes. That is the electoral democracy, the representative democracy enthusiastically defended by the representative of Colombia—the country where it is said that 200,000 to 300,000 people died as a result of the civil war that followed the death of Gaitán. And yet we are told there is nothing to liberate, there is nothing to avenge.

So apparently there are not thousands of deaths to be avenged, the army is not massacring the people, and this is not the same army that has been massacring the people since 1948. Apparently it has changed a bit, and the generals and the commanders are different, and the orders are different, and they are obeying a different class than the one that massacred the people during four long years of this struggle, and that has continued since then to massacre the people every so often. And the representative of Colombia says there is nothing to liberate.

Does the representative of Colombia not remember that in

Guevara during trip to Africa following his appearance at the United Nations. *Above,* press conference in Tanzania, February 18, 1965. At right is Pablo Rivalta Pérez, Cuba's ambassador to Tanzania; at left, Juan Rodríguez González.

Marquetalia there are forces that the Colombian newspapers themselves have called the "Independent Republic of Marquetalia," one of whose leaders has been nicknamed "Dead-eye Shot," to make him appear like a common bandit? Does he not know that a large military operation was carried out involving 16,000 Colombian troops, with U.S. military advisers, using helicopters and probably—although I cannot confirm it—U.S. aircraft as well? It seems the representative of Colombia is either badly informed as a result of being away from his country, or else he has a poor memory.

The representative of Colombia furthermore stated quite assuredly that had Cuba continued in the orbit of the Organization of American States, things would be different. We do not know what he meant by "orbit." Orbits are something that satellites have, and we are not a satellite. We are not in anyone's orbit—we are out of orbit. If we were in orbit, we naturally would have delivered here a honeyed speech, using very high-flown Spanish, full of fine adjectives. We would have spoken of the beauties of the inter-American system and of our firm and unshakable defense of the free world, directed by the center of that orbit—and everyone knows where that center is; I need not specify.

The representative of Venezuela also used a very moderate, though emphatic tone of voice. He stated that the charges of genocide were total slanders and that it was incredible that the Cuban government would involve itself in Venezuela's affairs when there is such repression in its own country.

We wish to state here a well-known fact, something we have always said to the world: yes, we shoot people, we have shot people, and we shall continue to shoot people as long as it is necessary. Our struggle is a struggle to the death. We know what the result would be if the battle were to be lost. These conditions have been imposed on us by U.S. imperialism.

But I must say this: we do not commit assassinations, such as the assassinations being committed at the present time by the Venezuelan political police—which, if I am not mistaken, is called Digepol. This police force has committed a series of barbarous acts such as executions and assassinations, dumping the bodies afterward. This has been used against students, among others. The free press of Venezuela has been suspended at various times recently for publishing news of this. Venezuelan military aircraft, with U.S. advisers, have also bombed large areas in the countryside, killing peasants. The popular rebellion in Venezuela is growing and we shall see the results before long.

The representative of Venezuela is indignant. I recall the indignation of the Venezuelan representatives when the Cuban delegation at Punta del Este read out loud the secret report that spokesmen of the United States of America were kind enough to send us—indirectly of course.[90] On that occasion we read aloud at the meeting in Punta del Este the U.S. government representatives' opinion of the Venezuelan government. They announced something extremely interesting. I don't have the exact quote in front of me, but it was to this effect: "Either these people will change or they will all face the firing squad." The "firing squad" is how they describe the Cuban revolution. The members of the U.S. embassy announced in irrefutable documents that this was the destiny of the Venezuelan oligarchy if it did not change its methods. They were accused of theft, and many other terrible accusations were made along these lines.

The Venezuelan delegation was extremely indignant. Naturally, it was not indignant at the United States; it was indignant at the Cuban delegation, which was good enough to read aloud the opinions of the United States about the government and people of Venezuela. The only result of all this was that Mr. Moscoso, who was gracious enough to make these documents available indirectly, was transferred to another post.

We remind the representative of Venezuela of this, to show that revolutions are not exportable. Revolutions happen, and the Venezuelan revolution will happen in its own time. And those who do not have an airplane ready—like in Cuba—to flee to Miami or elsewhere will have to face up to what the people decide. They will not be able to blame other governments for what happens.

I would like to recommend to the representative of Venezuela that he may, if he is interested, read some very interesting opinions about what guerrilla warfare is and how to combat it, written by some of the most intelligent elements of COPEI[91] and published in the Venezuelan press. He will see that one does not combat a people in arms with bombs and assassinations; that only makes the people more revolutionary. We know this very well. It is generally not a good idea to show one's declared enemy the strategy for countering guerrilla warfare; but we do so here knowing he is so blind he will not follow it.

We now come to Mr. Stevenson. Unfortunately, he is not here. We understand perfectly why he is not present. Once again we have heard his weighty and serious statements, so worthy of an intellectual of his stature. Equally emphatic, weighty, and serious statements were made by him in the First Committee on April 15, 1961, during Session 1149.

On that day U.S. pirate aircraft bearing Cuban markings had bombed Cuban airports and had almost knocked out our air force. These planes had come from Puerto Cabezas in Nicaragua, I recall, or perhaps from Guatemala—it was not made very clear. After cold-bloodedly carrying out their "great feat," the planes landed in the United States. When we denounced this act in the UN, Mr. Stevenson said some very interesting things.

I apologize for the length of these remarks, but I think it's worth recalling once again the weighty words of such a distinguished intellectual as Mr. Stevenson. These were made only four or five days before Mr. Kennedy calmly told the world that he assumed full responsibility for the events that had occurred in Cuba. I believe this is a summary, as we have not had time to obtain the transcripts of that meeting. Mr. Stevenson stated:

> The Cuban representative's charges against the United States concerning the bombing attacks reported to have been

carried out on the Havana and Santiago airports and on Cuban air force headquarters at San Antonio de los Baños are wholly unfounded.

—And Mr. Stevenson rejected them categorically.

As the president of the United States has said, there will not under any conditions be any intervention in Cuba by U.S. armed forces, and the United States will do everything in its power to make sure that no American participates in any actions against Cuba.

—A year later we were kind enough to return the remains of a pilot who fell in Cuban territory. Not Major Anderson; another one.

So far as the events which have purportedly occurred this morning and yesterday are concerned, the United States will consider requests for political asylum in accordance with its usual practices.

—That is, they are going to give political asylum to the people they themselves had sent.[92]

Those who believe in freedom and seek asylum from tyranny and oppression will always receive sympathetic understanding and consideration from the American people and the United States government.

Mr. Stevenson continued in this vein throughout his long oration.

Two days later, the members of Brigade 2506 landed at Playa Girón. Two days after that, this heroic brigade—whose heroism will surely go down in the annals of Latin American history—surrendered, with the loss of hardly a single man. Then began that charade you all know about, of men wearing the gusano[93] uniform they got from the U.S. Army all saying they were cooks, nurses, or sailors.

That was when President Kennedy made a worthy gesture. He did not attempt to maintain a farce that no one believed; he clearly stated that he assumed full responsibility for everything that had happened in Cuba. He took the responsibility, yes, but the Organization of American States did not assume any responsibility, so far as I remember. This responsibility was due to its own history and the history of the United States, because the Organization of American States was "in orbit." But the OAS did not have time to bother with these matters.

I am grateful to Mr. Stevenson for his historical reference to my long life as a communist and revolutionary, which has culminated in Cuba.[94] As always, United States agencies—both those of the press and of espionage—confuse things. My history as a revolutionary is a short one and it actually began with the *Granma* landing and has continued up to the present.

I did not belong to the Communist Party until I was in Cuba, and we can all proclaim before this assembly that the Cuban revolution follows Marxism-Leninism as its theory. What is important is not personal references. What is important is that Mr. Stevenson once again is saying that there was no violation of laws, that neither the planes nor the ships had left from the United States, that these pirate attacks had come from nowhere, that everything had come from nowhere.[95] He says all this with the same assurance, in the same calm and collected tone of voice of the intellectual that he used in 1961 when he stated emphatically that those "Cuban planes" had left from Cuban territory, and that the pilots were political exiles. Before being given the lie again, my distinguished colleague Mr. Stevenson thought it best to retire from this assembly hall.

The United States claims that it can carry out surveillance flights because the Organization of American States approved them. Who gave the Organization of American States the right to approve surveillance flights over a country's territory? What role does the United Nations play? Why do we have the United

Nations if our destiny is to depend on the "orbit," as the representative of Colombia so aptly put it, of the Organization of American States? This is a very serious and important question that we must bring before this assembly. Because we, a small country, cannot in any way agree to a big country having the right to violate our airspace, even if it uses the rather strange claim that its acts have the backing of the Organization of American States, an organization that expelled us and with which we have no connection whatsoever.

The representative of the United States has made some very serious statements. I would like to make only two small points. I do not wish to take up any more of the assembly's time with these replies and counter-replies.

The representative of the United States says that Cuba blames its economic disaster on the blockade, when it is really a consequence of bad management by the Cuban government.

When the first nationalization laws were instituted in Cuba, the United States began to take repressive economic actions, such as the unilateral cancellation of the sugar quota that we traditionally sold to the U.S. market. Similarly the United States refused to refine the petroleum we had bought from the Soviet Union, a purchase that was fully legitimate under every conceivable law.

I will not repeat the long history of U.S. economic aggression. But I will say that in spite of these aggressions and with the fraternal assistance of the socialist countries, especially the Soviet Union, we have made progress and will continue to do so. While we condemn the economic blockade, it will not stop us. No matter what happens, we will continue to be a small headache when we come to this assembly in order to call things by their right names, and to brand the United States as the instrument of repression throughout the world.

Finally, there is indeed an embargo on medicines to Cuba.[96] But if that is not the case, then in the coming months our government will place an order for medicines in the United States. And we will send a telegram to Mr. Stevenson, which our representative will read in the committee or wherever it is convenient, so that the truth of Cuba's charges can be verified. In any case, up to the present, these charges have been true. The last time we attempted to buy medicines, to the value of $1.5 million—medicines not manufactured in Cuba and that are necessary solely to save lives—the U.S. government intervened and prevented that sale.

A little while ago, the president of Bolivia told our representatives, with tears in his eyes, that he had to break relations with Cuba because the United States had forced him to do so. And because of this, our representatives had to leave La Paz. I cannot affirm that this assertion by the president of Bolivia was true; but what is true is that we told him that such deals with the enemy would be worth nothing because he was already condemned.

The president of Bolivia, with whom we did not and do not have any connection, and with whose government we had only the relations that are proper among the nations of Latin America, has since been overthrown by a military coup. A junta has now been established in Bolivia.

For such people, who do not know how to fall with dignity, it is worth recalling the words of the mother of the last caliph of Granada to her son, who was weeping over the loss of the city: "You do well to weep like a woman for what you did not know how to defend like a man."

I speak on behalf of the children
of the world who do not even
have a piece of bread

Fidel Castro

INTRODUCTORY NOTE

In October 1979 Castro addressed the United Nations General Assembly on behalf of the Movement of Nonaligned Countries.

Formed in 1961 with Cuba as a founding member, the Nonaligned Movement had grown by 1979 to include most former colonies and other countries dominated by imperialism. The Sixth Nonaligned Summit was held in Havana September 3–9, 1979. Present were delegations from 138 countries, including observers. Fifty-five heads of state attended.

As head of state of the host country, Castro assumed the organization's presidency for three years. In that capacity, he was responsible for reporting on the meeting's results to the United Nations.

The Sixth Summit met in the wake of tumultuous events and revolutionary victories that succeeded one after the other in 1979: in January the Pol Pot regime in Cambodia was ousted by the combined blows of an internal revolt and the intervention of the Vietnamese army; in February the shah of Iran was toppled by a mass revolutionary uprising; in March the Eric Gairy dictatorship in Grenada was overthrown and a popular revolutionary government established under the leadership of Maurice Bishop; and in July the Nicaraguan people, led by the Sandinista National Liberation Front, defeated the Somoza tyranny, giving impetus to a new upsurge of struggles throughout the region. These victories, and Cuba's guiding hand as the host country responsible for initiating resolutions, were reflected in the many strong anti-imperialist positions adopted by the meeting.

The U.S. government waged a concerted effort to undermine the Havana summit. It actively promoted efforts to have the meeting moved from Havana and to prevent Castro from assuming the presidency of the Nonaligned Movement. When that failed, it sought to pressure a number of governments not to attend. Several weeks before the summit was to open, Washington launched a widely publicized campaign charging the existence of a previously undetected "Soviet combat brigade" in Cuba. The accusation, which proved to be unfounded, was then dropped shortly after the Nonaligned summit meeting.

Castro's three-day visit to the United States—his first since 1960—included meetings with the UN secretary-general, diplomats from Nonaligned countries, members of the U.S. Congressional Black Caucus, and a number of journalists. He also met with Rafael Cancel Miranda, Lolita Lebrón, and Irving Flores, heroes of Puerto Rico's independence struggle who had been released from U.S. prisons the previous month after serving twenty-five-year sentences.

Castro's speech printed here was extensively publicized in the U.S. and world media. Substantial portions of his remarks were broadcast or quoted by the major television networks and newspapers.

Fidel Castro

I speak on behalf of the children of the world who do not even have a piece of bread

Address to General Assembly
October 12, 1979

Mr. President;
Distinguished representatives of the world community:

I have not come to speak about Cuba. I do not come to denounce before this assembly the aggressions to which our small but honorable country has been subjected for twenty years. Nor have I come to offend with unnecessary adjectives the powerful neighbor in his own house.

We have been charged by the Sixth Conference of Heads of State or Government of the Movement of Nonaligned Countries to present to the United Nations the results of its deliberations and the positions to be derived from them.

We are ninety-five countries from all continents, representing the immense majority of humanity. We are united by the determination to defend the cooperation between our countries, free national and social development, sovereignty, security, equality, and self-determination.

We are joined together in our determination to change the

present system of international relations, based as it is on injustice, inequality, and oppression. In international politics we act as an independent world factor.

Meeting in Havana, the Movement has just reaffirmed its principles and confirmed its objectives.

The Nonaligned countries stress that it is imperative to do away with the enormous inequality that separates the developed countries from the developing countries. We are struggling to eradicate poverty, hunger, disease, and illiteracy, from which hundreds of millions of human beings still suffer.

We aspire to a new world order, one based on justice, fairness, and peace. A new order that will replace the unjust and unequal system that prevails today, in which, as proclaimed in the final declaration of Havana, "wealth is still concentrated in the hands of a few powers whose wasteful economies are maintained by the exploitation of the labor as well as the transfer and plunder of the natural and other resources of the peoples of Africa, Asia, Latin America, and other regions of the world."

Among the problems to be debated in the present session of the General Assembly, peace is a concern of the first order. The search for peace also constitutes an aspiration of the Movement of Nonaligned Countries and was a subject of its attention at the Sixth Conference. But for our countries, peace is indivisible. We want a peace that will benefit equally the large and the small, the strong and the weak; a peace that will embrace all regions of the world and reach all its citizens.

Since its very inception the Movement of Nonaligned Countries has believed that the principles of peaceful coexistence should be the cornerstone of international relations. These principles should constitute the basis for the strengthening of peace and international security, for the relaxation of tensions, and for the expansion of that process to all regions of the world and to all aspects of international relations. They must be universally applied in relations among states.

But at the same time, the Sixth Summit believed that these principles of peaceful coexistence also include the right of peoples under foreign and colonial domination to self-determination. They include independence; sovereignty; the territorial integrity of states; the right of every country to put an end to foreign occupation and to the acquisition of territory by force; and the right to choose its own social, political, and economic system. Only in this way can peaceful coexistence be the foundation for all international relations.

This conclusion cannot be denied. When we analyze the structure of today's world, we see that these rights of our peoples are still not guaranteed. The Nonaligned countries know full well who our historic enemies are, where the threats come from, and how to combat them.

That is why in Havana we resolved to reaffirm that "the quintessence of the policy of nonalignment, in accordance with its original principles and essential character, involves the struggle against imperialism, colonialism, neocolonialism, apartheid, racism including Zionism, and all forms of foreign aggression, occupation, domination, interference, or hegemony, as well as against great-power and bloc policies."

Thus it will be understood that the final declaration of Havana also linked the struggle for peace with "political, moral, and material support for the national liberation movements and joint efforts to eliminate colonial domination and racial discrimination."

The Nonaligned countries have always attached great importance to the possibility and necessity of détente among the great powers. Thus the Sixth Conference pointed with great concern to the fact that in the period since the Colombo summit conference[97] there was a certain stagnation in the process of détente, which has continued to be limited "both in scope and geographically."

On the basis of that concern the Nonaligned countries— who have made disarmament and denuclearization one of the permanent and most prominent objectives of their struggle, and who took the initiative in the convocation of the Tenth Special Session of the General Assembly on Disarmament—

examined at their conference the results of the negotiations on strategic arms and the agreements known as SALT II.[98] They believe that these negotiations constitute an important step in the negotiations between the two main nuclear powers, and could open up prospects for more comprehensive negotiations leading to general disarmament and the relaxation of international tensions.

But as far as the Nonaligned countries are concerned, those treaties are only part of the road toward peace. Although negotiations between the great powers constitute a decisive element in the process, the Nonaligned countries once again reiterated that the effort to consolidate détente; to extend it to all parts of the world; and to avert the nuclear threat, the arms buildup, and war is a task in which all the peoples of the world must participate and exercise their responsibility.

Mr. President, basing ourselves on the concept of the universality of peace and on the need to link the search for peace, extended to all countries, with the struggle for national independence, full sovereignty, and full equality among states, we, the heads of state or government meeting at the Sixth Summit Conference in Havana, gave our attention to the most pressing problems in Africa, Asia, Latin America, and other regions.

It is important to stress that we started from an independent position not linked to policies that might stem from the contradiction between the great powers. If in spite of that objective and even-handed approach, our review of international events became a denunciation of the supporters of imperialism and colonialism, this merely reflects the essential reality of today's world.

Thus in analyzing the situation in Africa, the heads of state or government, while recognizing the progress made in the African peoples' struggle for their emancipation, stressed that the fundamental question of the region is the need to eradicate colonialism, racism, racial discrimination, and apartheid from the continent—particularly southern Africa.

It was indispensable for us to stress the fact that the colonialist and imperialist powers were continuing their aggressive policies with the aim of perpetuating, regaining, or extending their domination and exploitation of the African nations. That is precisely the dramatic situation in Africa. The Nonaligned countries could not fail to condemn the attacks on Mozambique, Zambia, Angola, and Botswana; the threats against Lesotho; the constant destabilization efforts in that area; and the role played by the racist regimes of Rhodesia and South Africa. The need for Zimbabwe and Namibia to rapidly achieve their full liberation is not just a cause of the Nonaligned countries or of the most progressive forces of our era. That objective is already contained in resolutions and agreements of the international community through the United Nations, and it implies duties that must be taken up, whose infractions must be denounced internationally.[99]

Therefore, when in the final declaration the heads of state or government approved the condemnation by name of a number of Western countries, headed by the United States, for their direct or indirect collaboration in the maintenance of racist oppression and South Africa's criminal policy, this did not involve even the slightest manifestation of ideological leaning. Nor was that the case when the declaration recognized the role played by the Nonaligned countries, the United Nations, the Organization of African Unity, the socialist countries, the Scandinavian countries, and other democratic and progressive forces in supporting the struggle of the peoples of Africa. All this was simply the faithful expression of objective reality. To condemn South Africa without mentioning those who make its criminal policies possible would have been incomprehensible.

More forcibly and urgently than ever, the Sixth Summit Conference expressed the need to end the denial of the Zimbabwean and Namibian peoples' right to independence, and of the pressing need of the Black men and women of South Africa to attain a status where they are considered as equal and respected human beings. The conference also expressed the need to guarantee conditions of peace and respect for all the countries of the region.

The continued support for the movements of national liberation, the Patriotic Front [of Zimbabwe] and SWAPO, was a decision that was as unanimous as it was expected.[100] And let us state very clearly here that this is not a case of expressing a unilateral preference for solutions through armed struggle. It is true that the conference praised the people of Namibia and SWAPO—their sole and authentic representative—for having intensified and advanced the armed struggle, and called for total and effective support for that form of combat. But that was due to the fact that the South African racists have slammed the door on any real negotiations, and to the fact that the efforts to achieve negotiated solutions went no further than mere maneuvers.

The attitude toward the Commonwealth's decisions at its Lusaka meetings last August to have the British government, as a legal authority in Southern Rhodesia, call a conference to discuss the problems of Zimbabwe, confirmed the fact that the Nonaligned countries are not opposed to solutions achieved without armed struggle, so long as they lead to the creation of an authentic majority government; so long as independence is achieved in a manner satisfactory to the fighting peoples; and so long as this is done in accordance with the resolutions of the Organization of African Unity, the United Nations, and our own Nonaligned countries.

Mr. President, the Sixth Summit once again had to express its regret over the fact that Resolution 1514 of the General Assembly of the United Nations, concerning the granting of independence to colonial countries and peoples, has not been applied to Western Sahara. We should recall that the decisions of the Nonaligned countries and the resolutions of the United Nations—particularly General Assembly Resolution 3331—have reaffirmed the inalienable rights of the people of Western Sahara to self-determination and independence.[101]

In this problem Cuba feels a very special responsibility, having participated in the United Nations commission that investigated the situation in Western Sahara. This enabled our representatives to verify the Saharawi people's total support for self-determination and independence.

We repeat here that the position of the Nonaligned countries is not one of antagonism against any country. The welcome we gave to the agreement between the Republic of Mauritania and the Polisario Front, and to Mauritania's decision to withdraw its forces from the territory of Western Sahara, is in keeping with the application of our principles and the agreements of the United Nations. This was also the case when we deplored the extension of Morocco's armed occupation of the southern part of Western Sahara, previously administered by Mauritania.

Therefore, the conference expressed its hope that the ad hoc committee established at the Sixteenth OAU Summit Conference would make it possible to ensure that the people of Western Sahara are allowed to exercise their right to self-determination and independence as rapidly as possible.

That same principle and stance determined the resolution on Mayotte and the Malagasy Islands and the need for them to be reintegrated into the Comoros and Madagascar respectively.[102]

Mr. President, there can be no doubt that the problem of the Middle East has become one of the situations of greatest concern in today's world. The Sixth Summit Conference examined it in its twofold dimension.

On the one hand the conference reaffirmed that Israel's determination to continue its policy of aggression, expansionism, and colonial settlement in the occupied territories—with the support of the United States—constitutes a serious threat to world peace and security. At the same time the conference examined the problem from the standpoint of the rights of the Arab countries and of the Palestinian question.

For the Nonaligned countries the Palestinian question is the very crux of the problem of the Middle East. These two problems form an integral whole and neither can be settled in isolation from the other.

No just peace can be established in the region unless it is based on the total and unconditional withdrawal by Israel from all the occupied Arab territories, as well as the return to the Palestinian people of all their occupied territories and the restoration of their inalienable national rights, including the right to return to their homeland, to self-determination, and to the establishment of an independent Palestinian state in accordance with Resolution 3236 of the General Assembly.[103]

This means that all measures taken by Israel in the occupied Palestinian and Arab territories—including the establishment of colonies or settlements on Palestinian land or other Arab territories, whose immediate dismantlement is a prerequisite for a solution of the problem—are illegal, null, and void.

As I stated in my address to the Sixth Summit:

> We are not fanatics. The revolutionary movement was always educated in hatred of racial discrimination and pogroms of any kind. From the bottom of our hearts, we repudiate the merciless persecution and genocide that the Nazis once unleashed on the Jews. But there is nothing in recent history that parallels it more than the dispossession, persecution, and genocide that imperialism and the Zionists are currently practicing against the Palestinian people.
>
> Pushed off their lands, expelled from their country, scattered throughout the world, persecuted and murdered, the heroic Palestinians are a moving example of selflessness and patriotism, living symbols of the greatest crime of our era.[104] [*Applause*]

No one should be surprised that the conference, for reasons stemming not from any political prejudice, but rather from an objective analysis of the facts, was obliged to point out the role of U.S. policy in the region. The U.S. government has aligned itself with Israel, supported it, and has worked to attain partial solutions favorable to Zionist aims and to guarantee the fruits of Israel's aggression at the expense of the Palestinian Arabs and the entire Arab nation. By so doing it has played a major role in preventing the establishment of a just and comprehensive peace in the region.

The facts, and only the facts, led the conference to condemn U.S. policies and maneuvers in that region.

When the heads of state or government arrived at a consensus condemning the Camp David agreement and the Egyptian-Israeli treaty of March 1979,[105] their formulations had been preceded by long hours of detailed study and fruitful exchanges. This allowed the conference to consider those treaties not only as a total abandonment of the cause of the Arab countries, but also as an act of complicity with the continued occupation of Arab territories.

These words are harsh, but they are true and just.

The Egyptian people are not the ones who were judged by the Movement of Nonaligned Countries. The Egyptian people command the respect of each and every one of our countries, and enjoy the solidarity of all our peoples. The same voices that were raised to denounce the Camp David agreements and the Egyptian-Israeli treaty praised Gamal Abdel Nasser, a founder of the Movement and an upholder of the fighting traditions of the Arab nation. No one will ever overlook Egypt's historic role in Arab culture and development, or of its merits as a founder and driving force in the Movement of Nonaligned Countries.

The conference also gave its attention to the problems of Southeast Asia. The growing conflicts and tensions in that region constitute a threat to peace that must be avoided.

Similar concern was expressed by the Sixth Summit regarding the situation of the Indian Ocean. The declaration adopted eight years ago by the United Nations General Assembly that the Indian Ocean should be a zone of peace has not been fulfilled. The military presence in the region has not been reduced but is growing. Military bases now extend as far as South Africa, and are also serving as a means of surveillance against the African liberation movements. The talks between the United States and the Soviet Union are still suspended, despite the recent agreement between the two countries to discuss their resumption. All this led the Sixth Summit Conference to invite all states concerned to work effectively to fulfill the objectives of the declaration of the Indian Ocean as a zone of peace.

The Sixth Conference analyzed other issues of regional and world interest, such as those touching on European security and cooperation. It also took up the problem of the Mediterranean, the tensions that still exist there and that have now increased as a result of Israel's aggressive policy and the support given it by certain imperialist powers.

The conference examined the question of Cyprus, an island still partially occupied by foreign troops, and of Korea, still divided despite the Korean people's desire for the peaceful reunification of their homeland. This led the Nonaligned countries to reaffirm and broaden resolutions of solidarity aimed at fulfilling the aspirations of both peoples.

It would be impossible to refer to all the political decisions of the Sixth Summit Conference. Doing so would prevent us from touching upon one of the most fundamental aspects of our Sixth Summit: its economic perspectives—the clamor of the people of the developing countries, weary as they are of their backwardness and the suffering it engenders. As the host country, Cuba will present to all members of the international community copies of the conference's final declaration and additional resolutions. But before relaying to you the Nonaligned countries' view of the world economic situation and what its demands and hopes are, permit me to take a few moments to inform you of the final declaration's approach to the questions facing Latin America at present.

The fact that the Sixth Conference was held in a Latin American country allowed the heads of state or government meeting there to recall that the peoples of that region began their efforts to obtain independence at the very beginning of the nineteenth century. They also did not forget, as it states in the declaration, that "Latin America is one of the regions of the world that historically has suffered from the aggression of United States and European imperialism, colonialism, and neocolonialism." The participants in the conference found it necessary to point out that remnants of colonialism, neocolonialism, and national oppression still remain in that land of struggle. Thus the conference called for the eradication of colonialism in all its forms and manifestations. It condemned the presence of foreign military bases in Latin America and the Caribbean, such as those in Cuba and Puerto Rico. And it demanded once again that the U.S. government and the other colonial powers return to those countries the part of their territory occupied by those bases against the will of their peoples.

The experience of other areas led the heads of state or government to reject and condemn the attempt to create in the Caribbean a so-called security force, a neocolonial mechanism incompatible with the sovereignty, peace, and security of these countries.

The conference called for the restitution of the Malvinas Islands to the Republic of Argentina, and reaffirmed its support for the inalienable right of the people of Belize to self-determination, independence, and territorial integrity.[106] In so doing, the conference once again gave evidence of what its declaration had defined as the very quintessence of nonalignment.

The conference welcomed the fact that as of October 1 [1979] the Panama Canal treaties concluded between the Republic of Panama and the United States would enter into effect.[107] It gave its full support to those treaties and called for fully respecting them in both letter and spirit. It also called on all the states of the world to adhere to the protocol of the treaty concerning the permanent neutrality of the Panama Canal.

The heads of state and government reiterated their solidarity with the struggle of the Puerto Rican people and that people's inalienable right to self-determination, independence, and territorial integrity. They did so despite the pressures, threats, cajoling, and stubborn opposition by the U.S. government in insisting that the issue of Puerto Rico be considered an internal question of the United States. And they called upon the government of the United States of America to refrain from any political or repressive maneuvers designed to perpetuate the colonial status of that country. [*Applause*]

No more appropriate tribute could be paid to Latin America's traditions of freedom and to the heroic people of Puerto Rico, who in recent days have just celebrated the anniversary of the "Cry of Lares," which some hundred years ago expressed their indomitable will for freedom.[108]

Referring to the Latin American reality, the heads of state or government, who had already analyzed the significance of the freedom struggle that took place in Iran, could not fail to mention the revolutionary upheaval in Grenada and the extraordinary victory of the people of Nicaragua and their vanguard, the Sandinista National Liberation Front, [*Applause*] emphasizing the enormous historical significance of that event for the peoples of Latin America and the world.[109] The heads of state or government also stressed something new in Latin American relations, something that sets an example for other regions of the world; namely the way in which the governments of Panama, Costa Rica, and Mexico, as well as the member countries of the subregional Andean Pact—Bolivia, Colombia, Ecuador, Peru, and Venezuela—acted in consort and solidarity to achieve a just solution to the Nicaraguan problem, as well as Cuba's traditional solidarity with the cause of that people.

I confess that these observations on Latin America alone would have justified the Cuban people's efforts and the work of the hundreds of thousands of our country's men and women to enable Cuba to give a worthy reception to the sister nations of the Movement of Nonaligned Countries at the Havana summit conference. But for Cuba there was much more; and on behalf of our people, we would like to acknowledge it from the rostrum of the United Nations.

The Havana conference also gave its support to the Cuban people's right to choose their political and social system; it called for returning the territory occupied by the Guantánamo base;

and it condemned the blockade by which the U.S. government continues its efforts to isolate the Cuban revolution, seeking to destroy it.[110] [*Applause*]

We appreciate the deep feeling and universal resonance of the Movement's recent denunciation in Havana of the hostile acts, pressures, and threats by the United States against Cuba, declaring these to be a flagrant violation of the United Nations Charter and the principles of international law, as well as a threat to world peace. Once again, we respond to our brothers, and we assure the international community that Cuba will remain true to the principles of international solidarity.

Mr. President, history has taught us that when a people freeing itself from a colonial or neocolonial system obtains its independence, it is both the last act in a long struggle and the first in a new and difficult battle. This is true because the independence, sovereignty, and freedom of our apparently free peoples are constantly threatened by foreign control over their natural resources, by financial impositions on the part of official international bodies, and by the precarious situation of their economies—all of which reduce their full sovereignty.

For this reason, at the very beginning of their analysis of world economic problems, the heads of state or government:

> Once again solemnly emphasized the paramount importance of consolidating political independence by economic emancipation. They therefore reiterated that the existing international economic system runs against the basic interests of developing countries, is profoundly unjust and incompatible with the development of the Nonaligned and other developing countries, and does not contribute to the elimination of the economic and social evils that afflict those countries.

And furthermore, they emphasized:

> the historic mission that the Movement of Nonaligned Countries should play in the struggle to attain the economic and

political independence of all developing nations and peoples, to exercise their full and permanent sovereignty and control over their natural and all other resources and economic activities, and to promote a fundamental restructuring of the world economy through the establishment of the new international economic order.

And the statement concludes with the following words:

The struggle to eliminate the injustice of the existing international economic system and to establish the new international economic order is an integral part of the people's struggle for political, economic, cultural, and social liberation.

It is not necessary to show here how profoundly unjust the existing international economic system is, and how incompatible it is with the development of the underdeveloped countries. The figures are already so well known that it is unnecessary to repeat them here.

There is a discussion about whether there are only 400 million undernourished people in the world or whether the figure has risen to 450 million, as certain international documents state. Four hundred million hungry men and women are already more than enough of an indictment.

What no one disputes is that all the hopes that have been raised in the developing countries appear to have been dashed and extinguished as this Second Development Decade ends.[111]

The director-general of the Food and Agricultural Organization council has acknowledged that "progress is still disappointingly slow in relation to the long-term development goals contained in the International Development Strategy, in the Declaration and the Program of Action on the Establishment of the New International Economic Order, and in the resolution of the World Food Conference and in several subsequent conferences." We are still far from having achieved the modest

4 percent annual average increase in the developing countries' food and agricultural production that was proposed ten years ago to solve some of the most pressing problems of world hunger and to approach consumption levels that are still quite low. As a result of this, food imports by the developing countries, which right now constitute a factor that aggravates their unfavorable balance of payments, will soon, according to FAO figures, reach unmanageable proportions. In the face of this, official commitments of foreign aid to agriculture in the developing countries are falling off.

This panorama cannot be prettied up. At times certain official documents reflect circumstantial increases in the agricultural production of some areas of the underdeveloped world, or stress the conjunctural price increases of some agricultural items. But these are cases of transitory progress and short-lived advantages.

The developing countries' agricultural export revenues are still unstable and insufficient to meet their import needs for food, fertilizers, and other items required to raise their own production. Per capita food production in Africa in 1977 was 11 percent below that of ten years earlier.

At the same time as backwardness in agriculture is perpetuated, the process of industrialization is not advancing either. And it cannot advance because the majority of the developed countries view the industrialization of the developing countries as a threat.

In 1975, the World Conference on Industrialization at Lima proposed as a goal that by the year 2000 the developing countries should produce 25 percent of the world's manufactured output. But the progress from the Lima conference up to today has been so insignificant that if the measures proposed by the Sixth Summit Conference are not implemented and if a crash program is not put into effect to modify the economic policies of the majority of the developed countries, that target will never be met. We now account for less than 9 percent of the world's manufactured output.

Our dependency is once again expressed in the fact that the countries of Asia, Africa, and Latin America import 26.1 percent of the manufactured goods that enter into international trade, while exporting only 6.3 percent of them. It may be said that some industrial expansion is taking place, but it does not take place at the necessary pace, nor in the key industries. This was pointed out at the Havana conference. The world redistribution of industry, the so-called industrial redeployment, should not consist of a reconfirmation of the deep economic inequalities that emerged during the colonial era of the nineteenth century. At that time we were condemned to be producers of raw materials and cheap agricultural products. Now an effort is being made to use the abundant labor power and starvation wages in the developing countries to transfer to them the low-technology industries, the industries of lowest productivity, and those that most pollute the environment. This we categorically reject.

The developed market-economy countries today absorb more than 85 percent of the world's high-technology industrial production. They also control more than 83 percent of all industrial exports; 26 percent of those exports go to the developing countries, whose markets they monopolize.

The most serious aspect of this dependent structure is that our imports—consumer items as well as capital goods—are all manufactured according to the demands, needs, and technology of the most developed industrial countries and the patterns of consumer societies, which are thus introduced through the cracks by way of our trade. In this way they contaminate our own societies and add a new element to the already permanent structural crisis.

The result of all this, as was noted by the heads of state or government in Havana, is that the gap between the developed and developing countries not only persists but has substantially increased. The relative share of the developing countries in world production output decreased considerably during the last two decades, with even more disastrous effects on such problems as malnutrition, illiteracy, and poor sanitary and health conditions.

Some would like to solve the tragic problem of humanity with drastic measures to reduce the population. They remember that wars and epidemics helped to reduce population in other eras. They wish to go even further; they want to blame underdevelopment on the population explosion.

The population explosion, however, is not the cause but the result of underdevelopment. Development will both bring solutions to the problems of poverty as well as help our countries, through education and culture, to attain rational and adequate rates of growth.

A recent report put out by the World Bank paints an even bleaker picture. It is possible, the report says, that by the year 2000 some 600 million people on this earth may still be submerged in absolute poverty.

Mr. President, distinguished representatives: The state of agricultural and industrial backwardness from which the developing countries have not managed to emerge is, as the Sixth Summit Conference pointed out, undoubtedly the result of unjust and unequal international relations. But, as the Havana declaration also points out, to this is now added the prolonged world economic crisis.

I shall not dwell too long on this aspect. Let us however state that we heads of state or government believe that the crisis of the international economic system is not conjunctural, but is rather a symptom of structural maladjustments and of a disequilibrium that are part of its very nature. We also believe that this disequilibrium has been aggravated by the refusal of the developed market-economy countries to control their external imbalances and their high rates of inflation and unemployment. And this inflation has been engendered precisely in those developed countries that refuse now to implement the only measures that could eliminate it. Let us also point out— and this is something we will return to later and that has also been set down in the Havana declaration—that this crisis is also the result of the persisting unfairness in international economic relations. Eliminating that inequality, as we propose, will contribute to reducing and eliminating the crisis itself.

What are the main conclusions formulated in Havana by the representatives of the Movement of Nonaligned Countries?

We condemn the persistent diversion of human and material resources into an arms race that is unproductive, wasteful, and dangerous to humanity. [*Applause*] And we demand that a substantial part of the resources now devoted to arms, particularly by the major powers, be used for economic and social development.

We expressed our grave concern over the negligible progress that has been made in the negotiations to implement the Declaration and the Program of Action on the Establishment of the New International Economic Order. We point out that this was due to the lack of political will on the part of the majority of the developed countries and we specifically censure the delaying, diversionary, and divisive tactics adopted by those countries. The failure of the Fifth Session of UNCTAD highlighted that situation.[112]

We observed that unequal exchange in international economic relations, defined as an essential characteristic of the system, has, if possible, become even more unequal. While the prices of manufactured products, capital goods, foodstuffs, and services that we import from the developed countries are constantly rising, the prices of the raw materials we export are stagnating and are subject to constant fluctuation. The terms of exchange have worsened. We emphasized that protectionism, one of the factors aggravating the Great Depression of the 1930s, has been reintroduced by some developed countries.

The conference expressed its regret that in the GATT negotiations the developed countries belonging to it did not take into account the interests and concerns of the developing countries, especially the least developed among them.[113]

The conference also denounced the way in which certain developed countries are intensifying their use of domestic subsidies for certain products, to the detriment of the products of the developing countries.

The conference deplored the shortcomings in the scope and operation of the Generalized System of Preferences.[114] In that spirit it condemned the discriminatory restrictions contained in the United States Foreign Trade Act and the inflexible positions adopted by some developed countries, which prevented the adoption of an agreement on these problems at the Fifth Session of UNCTAD.

We expressed our concern over the continual deterioration of the international monetary situation. The instability of the exchange rate of the main reserve currencies, along with inflation, increases the imbalance in the world economic situation and creates additional economic difficulties for the developing countries by lowering the real value of their export earnings and reducing the value of their foreign currency reserves.

We pointed out that the disorderly growth of international liquidity, mainly through the use of devalued United States dollars and other reserve currencies, is a negative factor. We noted that while the inequality of international economic relations is increasing the developing countries' accumulated foreign debt to over $300 billion, the international financial bodies and the private banks are raising their interest rates and imposing shorter terms of loan amortization, thus financially strangling the developing countries. The conference denounced all this as constituting an element of coercion in negotiations, allowing the developed countries to obtain additional political and economic advantages at the expense of our countries.

The conference took into account the neocolonialist effort to prevent the developing countries from exercising in a permanent and effective way their full sovereignty over their natural resources, and it reaffirmed this right. For the same reason it supported the efforts of raw-material-producing developing countries to obtain just and remunerative prices for their exports and to improve, in real terms, their export earnings.

Moreover, the conference paid more attention than ever to

the strengthening of economic relations and to scientific-technical and technological transfers among the developing countries. The concept of what could be defined as "collective self-reliance," that is, mutual support and collaboration among the developing countries, so that they depend first of all on their own collective forces, is given greater emphasis in the Havana declaration than ever before.

Cuba, as president of the Movement and as the coordinating country, intends, together with the Group of 77,[115] to do everything necessary to promote the Action Program outlined by the conference with regard to economic cooperation.

Nevertheless, we do not conceive of "collective self-reliance" as anything even remotely resembling self-sufficiency. We view it as a factor in international relations to marshal all the possibilities and resources of that considerable and important part of humanity represented by the developing countries and incorporate them in the general current of resources and economies that can be marshaled in both the capitalist camp and the socialist countries.

Mr. President, the Sixth Summit rejected the attempts of certain developed countries to try to use the question of energy to divide the developing countries.

The energy problem can be examined only in its historical context. We must take into account both the wasteful consumption patterns of some of the developed countries, which has led to the squandering of hydrocarbons, as well as the pillaging role of the transnational corporations—the beneficiaries until recently of cheap energy, which they have used irresponsibly. The transnationals simultaneously exploit both the producers and consumers, reaping unjustified windfall profits. At the same time they seek to blame the oil-exporting developing countries for the present situation.

Permit me to recall that in my opening remarks to the conference I pointed to the desperate situation of the non-oil-producing underdeveloped countries, especially the least developed ones. I expressed confidence that the Nonaligned oil-producing countries would find formulas to help alleviate the unfavorable situation of those countries that had already been hard hit by world inflation and the inequalities of trade relations, suffering serious balance-of-payments deficits and sharp increases in their foreign debts. But this does not obviate the principal responsibility of the developed countries, their monopolies, and their transnational corporations.

In considering the matter of energy from this standpoint, the heads of state or government stressed that this subject should be discussed in the context of international negotiations within the United Nations, with the participation of all countries and linking the energy question to all development questions, such as financial and monetary reforms, world trade, and raw materials. In this way a comprehensive and all-encompassing analysis can be made of those aspects linked to the establishment of a new international economic order.

Reviewing the main problems confronting the developing countries in the context of the world economy, we could not fail to examine the functioning of the transnational corporations. Once again their policies and practices were declared unacceptable. It was charged that in their search for profits they exhaust the resources, distort the economies, and violate the sovereignty of developing countries. They undermine the rights of peoples to self-determination and violate the principles of noninterference in the affairs of states. And they frequently resort to bribery, corruption, and other undesirable practices, through which they seek to subordinate, and do subordinate, the developing countries to the industrialized countries.

In view of the inadequate progress achieved in preparing a United Nations code of conduct to regulate the activities of transnational corporations, the conference reaffirmed the urgency of early completion of this work. The aim should be to provide the international community with a legal instrument with which to at least control and regulate the activities of the transnationals in accordance with the objectives and aspirations of the developing countries.

In setting forth all the overwhelming negative aspects of the economic situation of developing countries, the Sixth Summit called special attention to the mounting problems of the least developed and most disadvantaged countries, those that are landlocked and isolated. And it asked that urgent and special measures be adopted to alleviate their problems.

That, Mr. President and distinguished representatives, was the far from optimistic, rather somber and discouraging picture that the member countries of the Nonaligned Movement confronted when they met in Havana. But the Nonaligned countries did not allow themselves to be overcome by frustration or exasperation, however understandable that might have been. While drawing up strategic concepts for advancing their struggle, the heads of state or government repeated their demands and defined their positions.

The first fundamental objective in our struggle consists of reducing until we eliminate the unequal exchange that prevails today and converts international trade into a very useful vehicle for the plundering of our wealth. Today, one hour of labor in the developed countries is exchanged for ten hours of labor in the underdeveloped countries.

The Nonaligned countries demand that serious attention be paid to the Integrated Program for Commodities, which up until now has been manipulated and juggled in the so-called North-South negotiations. In the same way, we ask that the Common Fund, which was projected as an instrument of stabilization that would establish a permanent linkage between the prices we receive for our products and those paid for our imports, and which has barely begun to have an impact, be given a real boost.[116]

For the Nonaligned countries, such a linkage that permanently ties the prices of their export items with the prices of basic equipment, industrial products, raw materials, and technology that they import from the developed countries constitutes an essential pivot for all future economic negotiations.

The developing countries demand that the countries that have created inflation and have stimulated it through their policies adopt the necessary measures to control it, thus putting an end to the aggravation of the unequal exchange between our countries.

The developing countries demand—and will continue their struggle to achieve—access to the markets of the developed countries for the industrial products of their incipient economies. They demand a halt to the vicious protectionism that has been reintroduced into the international economy, and that threatens to once again lead us into a deadly economic war. They demand that the Generalized System of Nonreciprocal Tariff Preferences be applied generally and without deceptive falsehoods so that the young industries of the developing countries can produce without being crushed in the world market by the superior technological resources of the developed countries.

The Nonaligned countries believe that the negotiations about to be concluded on the Law of the Sea should not be used as certain developed countries seek to use them, that is, to ratify the existing imbalance regarding sea resources. They should be used instead as a vehicle for equitable redress. The Conference on the Law of the Sea has served once again to highlight the arrogance and imperialist determination of some countries. Placing their technological possibilities over and above the spirit of understanding and accommodation requested by the developing nations, these countries threaten to take unilateral action in carrying out deep-sea mining operations.[117]

The foreign debt of the developing countries has now risen to $335 billion. It is estimated that about $40 billion a year goes to servicing this foreign debt, which represents more than 20 percent of their annual exports. On the other hand, the average per capita income in the developed countries is now fourteen times that of the underdeveloped countries. This situation is no longer sustainable.

The developing countries need the establishment of a new system of financing, enabling them to obtain the necessary financial resources to ensure continuous and independent development of their economies. These financing methods should be long-term and low-interest. The use of these financial resources should be completely at the disposition of the developing countries. This will enable them to establish a system of economic priorities corresponding to their plans for industrial development. It will also help prevent those funds from being absorbed, as they are today, by the transnational corporations, which use alleged financial contributions for development to aggravate the distortions of the developing countries' economies and reap maximum profits from the exploitation of these countries' resources.

The developing countries, and on their behalf the Movement of Nonaligned Countries, demand that a substantial portion of the immense resources now being squandered by humanity on the arms race be dedicated to development. This in turn would contribute to reducing the danger of war and helping improve the international situation.

The Nonaligned countries, expressing the position of all the developing countries, demand the establishment of a new international monetary system, which would stop the disastrous fluctuations now experienced by the main currencies used in the international economy, particularly the U.S. dollar. The financial disorder also hits the developing countries hard. And they hope that in drawing up the new international monetary system, they—as the majority of the countries in the international community, representing more than 1.5 billion men and women—may be given a voice and vote.

Summing up, Mr. President, distinguished representatives:

Unequal exchange is ruining our peoples. It must end!

Inflation, which is being exported to us, is crushing our peoples. It must end!

Protectionism is impoverishing our peoples. It must end!

The existing imbalance in the exploitation of the resources

of the sea is abusive. It must be abolished!

The financial resources received by the developing countries are insufficient. They must be increased!

Arms expenditures are irrational. They must cease and the funds thus released must be used to finance development!

The international monetary system prevailing today is bankrupt. It must be replaced!

The debts of the least-developed countries, and of those in a disadvantageous position, are burdens impossible to bear, to which no solution can be found. They must be cancelled! [*Applause*]

Indebtedness oppresses the rest of the developing countries economically. There must be relief!

The economic chasm between the developed countries and the countries seeking development is not narrowing but widening. It must be closed!

These are the demands of the underdeveloped countries.

Mr. President, distinguished representatives: Response to these demands, some of which have been systematically presented by the developing countries in international forums, through the Group of 77 and the Movement of Nonaligned Countries, would permit a change of course in the international economic situation. It would provide the developing countries with the institutional conditions for organizing programs that would definitively place them on the road to development.

But even if all these measures were implemented, even if all the mistakes and evils of the present system of international relations were corrected, the developing countries would still lack one decisive element: external financing.

All the domestic efforts, all the sacrifices that the peoples of the developing countries are making and are willing to make, and all the opportunities for increasing the economic potential that could be achieved by eliminating the inequality between the prices of their exports and of their imports, and by improving the conditions in which their foreign trade is carried out, would nevertheless not be sufficient.

In the light of their true financial situation at present, these countries need further resources to be able both to pay their debts and to make the enormous expenditures required on a world level for the leap into development. Here again, the figures are far too well known to require repeating.

The Sixth Summit Conference was concerned not only because the debts of the underdeveloped countries are practically unbearable, but also because the debt is growing yearly at a rate that could be termed galloping. The data contained in the recent World Bank report, which came out while we were holding the conference in Havana, confirmed that the situation is growing worse every day. In 1978 alone, the foreign public debt of ninety-six of the developing countries rose by $51 billion. This rate of growth has raised the foreign debt to the astronomical figures already mentioned.

We cannot, Mr. President, resign ourselves to this somber prospect.

The most renowned economists, both Western and those who ascribe to Marxist concepts, admit that the system of international indebtedness of the developing countries is completely irrational. And they acknowledge that its persistence could lead to a sudden interruption that might endanger the entire precarious and unstable world economic equilibrium.

Some try to explain the surprising economic fact that the international banking centers continue to provide funds to countries that are technically bankrupt, arguing that these are generous contributions to help those countries meet their economic difficulties. But this is not so. It is, in fact, an operation to save the international capitalist order itself. In October 1978, the Commission of European Communities admitted by way of clarification:

> The present equilibrium of the world economy depends to a considerable extent on continuing the flow of private loans to non-oil-producing developing countries . . . on a scale unprec-

edented prior to 1974, and any obstacle to that flow will endanger this equilibrium.

World financial bankruptcy would be very hard, most of all for the underdeveloped countries and the workers in the developed capitalist countries. It would also affect even the most stable socialist economies. But it is doubtful that the capitalist system would be able to survive such a catastrophe. And it would be difficult for the terrible economic situation that results not to inevitably engender a world conflagration. There is already talk of special military forces to occupy the oil fields and the sources of other raw materials.

But if it is the duty of everyone to be concerned over this somber prospect, it is first of all the duty of those who possess the greatest wealth and material abundance.

In any case, the prospect of a world without capitalism is not too frightening to us revolutionaries. [*Laughter and applause*]

It has been proposed that instead of a spirit of confrontation we employ a sense of world economic interdependency that will enable us to utilize the resources of all our economies to obtain joint benefits. But the concept of interdependency is acceptable only when one starts by admitting the intrinsic and brutal injustice of the present interdependency.

The developing countries reject those who present "interdependency" as the unjust, arbitrary international division of labor imposed on them by modern colonialism, beginning with the English industrial revolution, and deepened by imperialism.

If we wish to avoid confrontation and struggle, which seems to be the only road open to the developing countries—a road that offers long and arduous battles whose proportions no one today can predict—then we must all seek and find formulas for cooperation to solve the great problems. These problems, although they affect our peoples, cannot be solved without also affecting the most developed countries in one way or another.

Not so many years ago we stated that the irrational squandering of material goods and the subsequent waste of economic resources by developed capitalist society had already become unsustainable. Is that not the cause of the dramatic energy crisis that we now face? And who, if not the non-oil-producing underdeveloped countries, has to bear the main brunt of it?

These views on the need to put an end to the wastefulness of the consumer societies is very widely held. A recent document of the United Nations Industrial Development Organization states, "The present way of life, especially in the industrialized countries, may have to undergo a radical and painful change."

Naturally, the developing countries cannot and do not expect that the transformation they seek and the financing they require will be given them as a gift, coming as a result of a mere analysis of international economic problems. In this process, which implies contradictions, struggles, and negotiations, the Nonaligned countries must first of all depend upon their own determination and efforts.

That conviction emerges clearly from the Sixth Summit Conference. In the economic part of the final declaration, the heads of state or government recognize the need to carry out the necessary economic and social structural changes in their own countries, believing this to be the only way of eliminating the present vulnerability of their economies and of turning a simple statistical growth into genuine development.

Only in this way, the heads of state and government recognize, will their peoples be willing to pay the price required of them to become the main protagonists in the process. As I said on that occasion, "If the system is socially just, the possibilities of survival and economic and social development are incomparably greater." The history of my own country provides irrefutable proof of this.

The emerging and crying need to solve the problem of underdevelopment brings us back, Mr. President, to the problem I mentioned a little while ago, and which is the last one I should like to submit to this Thirty-fourth Session of the General Assembly. I refer to the question of international financing.

Supporters of the Cuban revolution demonstrate outside the UN to welcome Castro during his 1979 visit.

As we have already said, one of the most serious phenomena accompanying the accelerated indebtedness of the developing countries is that most of the funds received from abroad by the developing nations are earmarked to cover their trade balances and negative current accounts, to renew their debts, and to make interest payments.

If we take as an example the non-oil-exporting developing countries, whose situation I referred to at the Havana conference, we note that in the last six years alone they have run up deficits in their balance of payments of over $200 billion.

In view of this, the investments required by the developing countries are enormous. And they are needed primarily, and almost exclusively, in precisely those branches of production that yield low profits and therefore do not attract private foreign lenders or investors.

To increase the production of foodstuffs in order to eliminate the malnutrition that afflicts the 450 million persons I mentioned earlier, new land and water resources must be provided. According to the estimates of specialists, in the next ten years 76 million additional hectares of land in the developing countries would have to be cultivated, and over 10 million additional hectares of land irrigated, to meet these needs.

Irrigation systems for 45 million hectares of land would have to be repaired. And therefore, even the most modest estimates admit—and I refer to aid, not the total flow of resources—that between $8 billion and $9 billion a year will be required in international financial aid to obtain an agricultural growth rate of 3.5 to 4 percent in the developing countries.

With regard to industrialization, the estimates are far higher. At its meeting in Lima the United Nations Conference on Industrial Development, in defining the goals we mentioned earlier, stated that at the heart of international development policy is financing. It stated that by the year 2000 there will need to be annual levels of financing of $450 billion to $500 billion, of which a third—that is, from $150 billion to $160 billion—will have to be financed from external sources.

But development, Mr. President and distinguished represen-tatives, includes more than agriculture and industrialization. Development primarily involves attention to human beings, who should be the protagonists and goal of all development efforts.

To cite the example of Cuba, I will point out that during the last five years our country has invested an average of nearly $200 million a year in school construction. Investment in medical equipment and construction of public health facilities has averaged over $40 million a year. And Cuba is only one of nearly a hundred developing countries, and one of the smallest in terms of geography and population. From this it can be estimated that the developing countries will need tens of billions of dollars more invested every year in education and public health services to overcome the results of backwardness.

That is the great problem that faces us.

And this, gentlemen, is not our problem alone, a problem solely for the countries victimized by underdevelopment and insufficient development. It is a problem for the international community as a whole.

On more than one occasion it has been stated that we were forced into underdevelopment by colonization and imperialist neocolonization. The task of helping us to emerge from under-development is therefore first and foremost a historic and moral obligation of those who benefited from the plunder of our wealth and the exploitation of our men and women over decades and centuries. [*Applause*] But it is at the same time the task of hu-manity as a whole, as was stated at the Sixth Summit Confer-ence.

The socialist countries did not participate in the plunder of the world, nor are they responsible for the phenomenon of underdevelopment. But even so, because of the nature of their social system, in which internationalist solidarity is a premise, they understand and assume the obligation of helping to over-come it.

Likewise, when the world expects the oil-producing developing countries to contribute to the universal flow of external financing for development, it does not present this as a historic obligation and duty—which no one can impose—but as a hope and a duty of solidarity among underdeveloped countries. The big oil-exporting countries should be aware of their responsibilities.

Even the developing countries that are relatively more advanced should make their contributions. Cuba, which is not speaking here on behalf of its own interests and is not defending national objectives, is willing to contribute, in accordance with its means, thousands or tens of thousands of technicians, doctors, teachers, agronomists, hydraulic engineers, mechanical engineers, economists, middle-level technicians, skilled workers, and so on.

The time has therefore come for all of us to join in the task of drawing entire peoples, hundreds of millions of human beings, out of the backwardness, poverty, malnutrition, disease, and illiteracy that keep them from enjoying full human dignity and pride. [*Applause*]

We must therefore marshal our resources for development, and this is our joint obligation.

Mr. President, there are many special multilateral funds, both public and private, whose purpose is to contribute to one or another aspect of development, whether agricultural or industrial, or for meeting balance-of-payments deficits. Therefore it is not easy for me, in presenting to this Thirty-fourth Session of the General Assembly a report on the economic problems discussed at the Sixth Summit Conference, to formulate a concrete proposal for the establishment of a new fund.

But there can be no doubt that the problem of financing should be discussed thoroughly and fully in order to find a solution to it. In addition to the resources already gathered by various banking channels, loan organizations, international bodies, and private finance agencies, we must discuss and decide upon a strategy for the next Development Decade that will include an additional contribution of not less than $300 billion at 1977 real value, to be invested in the underdeveloped countries and to be made in yearly installments of at least $25 billion from the very beginning. [*Applause*] This aid should be in the form of donations and long-term, low-interest credits.

It is imperative that these additional funds be gathered as a contribution to the underdeveloped world by the developed world and other countries with resources over the next ten years. If we want peace, these resources will be required. If there are no resources for development, there will be no peace. Some may think that we are asking too much. But I believe that the figure is still modest. According to statistical information, as I stated at the opening session of the Sixth Summit Conference of Nonaligned Countries, the world annually invests more than $300 billion in military expenditures.

With $300 billion it would be possible to build 600,000 schools with a capacity for 400 million children; 60 million comfortable homes for 300 million people; 30,000 hospitals with 18 million beds; 20,000 factories with jobs for more than 20 million workers; or it would be possible to build irrigation systems to water 150 million hectares of land, which, with appropriate technology, could feed a billion people. Humanity wastes this much every year on its military spending.

Moreover, consider further the enormous waste of youthful human resources, of technicians, of scientists, of fuel, raw materials, and other items. This is the fabulous price we pay for the lack of a true climate of trust and peace in the world.

The United States alone will spend six times this amount on military activities in the 1980s.

We are requesting less for ten years of development than is spent in a single year by the ministries of war, and much less than a tenth of what will be spent for military purposes in ten years.

Some may consider our demand irrational. But what is truly irrational is the world's madness in our era and the perils that threaten humanity.

The enormous responsibility of studying, organizing, and

distributing these amounts of resources should be entrusted entirely to the United Nations. These funds should be administered by the international community itself on a footing of absolute equality for all countries, whether they are contributors or beneficiaries, without any political conditions, and without the amount of the donations having anything to do with the voting power to decide when and to whom loans are to be granted.

Even though the flow of resources should be measured in financial terms, it should not consist only of money. It may well be made up of equipment, fertilizer, raw materials, fuel, and complete factories valued in the terms of international trade. Aid in the form of technical personnel and the training of technicians should also be considered a contribution and counted as such.

We are convinced, Mr. President and distinguished representatives, that if the secretary-general of the United Nations, assisted by the president of the General Assembly and the prestige and weight of this organization, and supported further from the outset by the developing countries and especially the Group of 77—we are convinced that if he were to draw together the various factors we have mentioned to initiate discussions—in which there would be no room for so-called North-South, East-West antagonisms, but instead where all forces would join in a common undertaking, a common duty, a common hope—then this idea that we now submit to the General Assembly could be crowned with success.

This is not a project that will benefit only the developing nations. It will benefit all countries.

As revolutionaries we are not afraid of confrontation. We have placed our trust in history and peoples. But as spokesman and interpreter of the feelings of ninety-five countries, we have the responsibility to fight for cooperation among peoples. This cooperation, built on a new and just basis, will benefit all countries comprising the international community today. And it will especially benefit the prospects for world peace.

In the short term, development may well be a task entailing apparent sacrifices and even donations that may seem irrecoverable. But the vast world now submerged in backwardness, with no purchasing power and extremely limited consumer capacity will, as it develops, add a flood of hundreds of millions of consumers and producers. This is the only way that the international economy can be rehabilitated, including the economies of the developed countries that today engender and suffer from economic crisis.

The history of international trade has shown that development is the most dynamic factor in world trade. A major portion of trade at present takes place among fully industrialized countries. We can assure you that as industrialization and progress spread throughout the world, so too will trade, to the benefit of all.

It is for this reason that on behalf of the developing countries we advocate our cause and ask you to support it. But this is not a gift we seek from you. If we do not come up with effective solutions, we will all be victims of the catastrophe.

Mr. President, distinguished representatives:

Human rights are often spoken of, but we must also speak of humanity's rights.

Why should some people go barefoot, so that others may travel in expensive cars?

Why should some live only thirty-five years, so that others may live seventy?

Why should some be miserably poor, so that others may be exaggeratedly rich?

I speak on behalf of the children of the world who do not even have a piece of bread. [*Applause*] I speak on behalf of the sick who lack medicine. I speak on behalf of those who have been denied the right to life and to human dignity.

Some countries are on the sea, others are not. [*Applause*] Some have energy resources, others do not. Some possess abundant land on which to produce food, others do not. Some are so glutted with machinery and factories that even the air cannot be breathed because of the poisoned atmosphere, [*Applause*] while others have only their own emaciated arms with which to earn their daily bread.

In short, some countries possess abundant resources, others have nothing. What is their fate? To starve? To be eternally poor?

Why then civilization? Why then the conscience of man? Why then the United Nations? [*Applause*] Why then the world?

One cannot speak of peace on behalf of tens of millions of human beings all over the world who are starving to death or dying of curable diseases. One cannot speak of peace on behalf of 900 million illiterates.

The exploitation of the poor countries by the rich countries must cease!

I know that in many poor countries there are both exploiters and exploited.

I address myself to the rich nations, asking them to contribute. And I address myself to the poor nations, asking them to distribute.

Enough of words! We need deeds! [*Applause*]

Enough of abstractions! We need concrete action!

Enough of speaking about a speculative new international economic order that nobody understands. [*Laughter and applause*] We must speak of a real, objective order that everybody understands!

I have not come here as a prophet of revolution. I have not come here to ask or to wish that the world be violently convulsed. I have come to speak of peace and cooperation among the peoples. And I have come to warn that if we do not peacefully and wisely resolve the present injustices and inequalities, the future will be apocalyptic. [*Applause*]

The sounds of weapons, of threatening language, and of prepotent behavior on the international arena must cease. [*Applause*]

Enough of the illusion that the problems of the world can be solved by nuclear weapons. Bombs may kill the hungry, the sick, and the ignorant; but they cannot kill hunger, disease, and ignorance. Nor can they kill the righteous rebellion of the peoples. And in the holocaust, the rich—who have the most to lose in this world—will also die. [*Applause*]

Let us say farewell to arms, and let us in a civilized manner dedicate ourselves to the most pressing problems of our times. This is the responsibility and the most sacred duty of all the world's statesmen. This, moreover, is the basic premise for human survival.

I thank you. [*Ovation*]

Appendix

Fidel Castro's arrival in Harlem

The Cuban delegation hosts a luncheon for workers at the Hotel Theresa, attended by members of the press. At Castro's left is Juan Almeida.

Fidel Castro's arrival in Harlem

One event that occurred during Castro's 1960 visit to the United States was a meeting between two of the outstanding twentieth-century revolutionary leaders of the Americas— Fidel Castro and Malcolm X.

The discussion took place at the Hotel Theresa in Harlem, shortly after the Cuban delegation's arrival on the evening of September 19. As Castro stated thirty years later: "I will always recall my meeting with Malcolm X at the Hotel Theresa, because he was the one who made it possible and gave his support so that we could stay there. We had two alternatives [of places to stay]. One was the United Nations gardens. When I mentioned this to the secretary-general, he was horrified at the thought of a delegation in tents there. But then we received Malcolm X's offer—he had spoken with one of our compañeros. And I said, 'That is the place, the Hotel Theresa.' And there we went."

At the time Malcolm X was the leading spokesman of the Nation of Islam in New York. In March 1964, he broke with that organization. Less than a year later, in February 1965, he was assassinated.

Commenting on the meeting, Malcolm X told the press, "Premier Castro has come out against lynching, which is more than President Eisenhower has done. Castro has also taken a more open stand for civil rights for Black Cubans."

Malcolm X met with Castro as a prominent member of a "welcoming committee" that had been set up in Harlem several weeks earlier. The purpose of this group, which included a wide range of Black community leaders, was to greet heads of state, particularly from African countries, who would be in New York to address the UN General Assembly. Sixteen African countries were admitted to membership in the UN at that session.

Malcolm X came under attack in the media for his initiative in welcoming the Cuban delegation and for taking responsibility for the organization of a defense guard at the Hotel Theresa to assure their safety. When prominent members of the Welcoming Committee refused to support Malcolm's stand, he publicly resigned from that body. "During the time Dr. Castro was in Harlem, thanks to the Nationalists and the Muslims, there was no rioting or lawlessness in Harlem," Malcolm X wrote. "The Muslims and the Black Nationalists in Harlem exerted every imaginable effort to see that Harlem remained 'calm and orderly.'"

"Despite this," he continued, "the daily press has unleashed a savage propaganda attack against us, purposely distorting facts, purposely telling bare-faced lies, labeling us as lawless terrorists, subversives, seditionists, etc." In resigning from the Welcoming Committee, Malcolm pledged to "henceforth confine my activities and efforts with and among the little men in the street, whose honesty and integrity makes them fearless when time comes to take an uncompromising stand, without hesitation, on the side of right and truth."

The article printed here is an account of the meeting between Castro and Malcolm X, written by Ralph D. Matthews, one of the journalists present. It was published in the September 24, 1960, *New York Citizen-Call.*

UP IN FIDEL'S ROOM

To see Premier Fidel Castro after his arrival at Harlem's Hotel Theresa meant getting past a small army of New York City policemen guarding the building, past security officers, U.S. and Cuban. But one hour after the Cuban leader's arrival, Jimmy Booker of the *Amsterdam News,* photographer Carl Nesfield, and myself were huddled in the stormy petrel of the Caribbean's room listening to him trade ideas with Muslim leader Malcolm X.

Dr. Castro did not want to be bothered with reporters from the daily newspapers, but he did consent to see two representatives from the Negro press.

Malcolm X gained entry when few others could because he had recently been named to a welcoming committee for visiting dignitaries set up by Harlem's Twenty-eighth Police Precinct Council.[118]

We followed Malcolm and his aides, Joseph and John X, down the ninth-floor corridor. It was lined with photographers disgruntled because they had no glimpse of the bearded Castro, with writers vexed because security men kept pushing them back.

We brushed by them and, one by one, were admitted to Dr. Castro's suite. He rose and shook hands with each one of us in turn. He seemed in a fine mood. The rousing Harlem welcome still seemed to ring in his ears.

Castro was dressed in green army fatigues. I expected them to be as sloppy as news photos tended to make them. To my surprise, his casual attire, just the same was immaculately creased and spanking clean.

His beard by dim room light was dark brown with just a suggestion of red.

After introductions, he sat on the edge of the bed, bade Malcolm X sit beside him, and spoke in his curious brand of broken English. His first words were lost to us assembled around him. But Malcolm heard him and answered: "Downtown for you it was ice. Uptown it is warm."

The premier smiled appreciatively. "Aahh yes. We feel here very warm."

Then the Muslim leader, ever a militant, said, "I think you will find the people in Harlem are not so addicted to the propaganda they put out downtown."

In halting English, Dr. Castro said, "I admire this. I have seen how it is possible for propaganda to make changes in people. Your people live here and they are faced with this propaganda all the time and yet they understand. This is very interesting."

"There are twenty million of us," said Malcolm X, "and we always understand."

Members of the Castro party spilled over from an adjoining room, making the small quarters even more cramped. Most of the Cubans smoked long cigars and when something amused them, they threw their heads back and blew smoke puffs as they laughed.

Castro's conversational gestures were unusual. He would touch his temples with extended fingers as he made a point or tapped his chest as if to see if it were still there.

His interpreter would translate longer sentences from Malcolm X into Spanish and Castro would listen alertly and smile courteously.

During the course of their conversation, Cuba's Castro and Harlem's Malcolm covered much political and philosophical ground.

On his troubles with the Hotel Shelburne, Dr. Castro said: "They have our money. Fourteen thousand dollars. They didn't want us to come here. When they knew we were coming here, they wanted to come along." (He did not clarify who "they" was in this instance.)

On racial discrimination: "We work for every oppressed person." But he raised a cautioning hand. "I did not want to interfere in the inner policy of a country."

And then in a slight voice of warning, still on the general theme of racial inequity, Dr. Castro said, "I will speak in the Hall (referring to the United Nations General Assembly)."

On Africa:

"Is there any news on Lumumba?" Malcolm X smiled broadly at the mention of the Congolese leader's name. Castro then raised his hand. "We will try to defend him (Lumumba) strongly."

"I hope Lumumba stays here at the Theresa."

"There are fourteen African nations coming into the Assembly. We are Latin Americans. We are their brothers."

On American Negroes:

"Castro is fighting against discrimination in Cuba, everywhere."

"You lack rights and you want your rights."

"Our people are changing. Now we're one of the most free people in the world."

"Negroes in the U.S. have more political conscience, more vision than anyone else."

On U.S.-Cuban relations: In answer to Malcolm's statement that "As long as Uncle Sam is against you, you know you're a good man," Dr. Castro replied, "Not Uncle Sam, but those here who control magazines, newspapers . . . "

On the UN General Assembly: "There will be a tremendous lesson to be learned at this session. Many things will happen in this session and the people will have a clearer idea of their rights."

Dr. Castro tapered the conversation off with an attempted quote of Lincoln. "You can fool some of the people some of the time, . . . " but his English faltered and he threw up his hands as if to say, "You know what I mean."

Malcolm, rising to leave, explained his Muslim group for a Cuban reporter who had just come in, "We are followers of

Muhammad. He says we can sit and beg for 400 more years. But if we want our rights now, we will have to . . . " Here he paused and smiled enigmatically, "Well, . . . "

Castro smiled. He smiled again as Malcolm told him a parable. "No one knows the master better than his servants. We have been servants ever since we were brought here. We know all his little tricks. Understand? We know what he is going to do before he does."

The Cuban leader listened to this being translated into Spanish, then threw his head back and laughed heartily. "Sí," he said heartily. "Sí."

We said our adios and then walked down the crowded hall, took the elevator to the street, where outside the crowds still milled around.

Some excited Harlemite then shouted into the night, "Viva Castro!"

Militant

Cuban leaders Juan Almeida and Antonio Núñez at Harlem coffeeshop, September 1960.

Notes

1. Shortly before Angola's independence from Portuguese colonial rule was to be formally celebrated on November 11, 1975, the country's new government—led by the Popular Movement for the Liberation of Angola (MPLA)—was attacked by South African and Zairean troops. The invading forces were allied with the Angolan National Liberation Front (FNLA) and the Union for the Total Independence of Angola (UNITA).

2. In early 1988 combined Cuban, Angolan, and Namibian forces dealt a decisive military defeat to South Africa's invading troops at Cuito Cuanavale in southern Angola. South Africa then opened negotiations leading to an accord signed in December 1988 in which Pretoria agreed to withdraw from Namibia. Describing Cuba's attitude toward the battle at Cuito Cuanavale, Fidel Castro said, "Our country staked everything by sending its best weapons and over 50,000 men." For Cuba, he said, "everything was on the line, including the revolution." (Fidel Castro, speech to Council of State, July 9, 1989, in *Granma*, July 12, 1989. This speech was also printed in *Granma Weekly Review*, July 23, 1989, and the *Militant*, August 11, 1989.)

3. Following the victory of the Cuban revolution in 1959, a number of leading figures in the regime of dictator Fulgencio Batista fled to the United States, including many of its most notorious torturers and murderers within the army and police.

4. On September 21, 1960, a few days after the arrival of the Cuban delegation in the United States, a fight took place in a Manhattan restaurant between Cuban supporters and opponents of the revolution. Shots were fired, and a bystander in the restaurant, a nine-year-old girl from Venezuela, was hit by a stray bullet; she died the following day. The New York police announced that the shot had been fired by a supporter of the revolution, and this version was publicized extensively by the media. On October 14, Francisco Molina, a Cuban immigrant and supporter of the revolution, was arrested and charged with murder. Molina was convicted and sentenced to twenty-years-to-life imprisonment. He was later freed

and sent to Cuba in exchange for the release of a counterrevolutionary prisoner by the Cuban government.

5. The tenor of this press campaign, based on "reports" and "stories" by anonymous sources, can be gauged from the article that appeared in the September 25 *New York Journal-American*. The article reported on accounts of women "cavorting inside the hotel." It stated: "There were stories of gay parties with New York blondes and dark-eyed Latin senoritas visiting the suites of the Cuban UN delegation at all hours of the day and night." The rest of the article went on to describe "reports of liquor flowing freely far into the night" and accounts of "Cubans living it up with plenty of feminine company."

6. *The Respectful Prostitute* is the title of a 1946 play by Jean-Paul Sartre.

7. From 1868 to 1898 Cubans waged three wars for independence from Spain. The first, the Ten Years War, lasted from 1868 until 1878. The second, known as the "Little War," occurred in 1879–80. The final war for independence was fought from 1895 to 1898, leading to the end of Spanish colonial rule. It was immediately followed, however, by a U.S. military occupation of the country.

8. In 1823 President John Quincy Adams wrote: "There are laws of politics as well as of physical gravitation, and if an apple, severed by a tempest from its native tree, cannot choose but fall to the ground, Cuba, forcibly disjoined from its own unnatural connexion with Spain, and incapable of self-support, can gravitate only toward the North American Union, which, by the same law of nature, cannot cast her off from its bosom."

9. The joint resolution passed April 20, 1898, gave the U.S. president authority to use military measures to force Spain to relinquish its authority over Cuba. In what became known in the United States as the Spanish-American War, U.S. forces seized Spain's colonies of Cuba, Puerto Rico, Guam, and the Philippines.

10. The Platt Amendment was drafted by U.S. Sen. Orville Platt and incorporated into the Cuban constitution in 1901. The amendment granted Washington the right to intervene in Cuban affairs at any time and to establish military bases on Cuban soil. The Platt Amendment was abrogated in 1934 under a treaty signed by both governments, which legalized all concessions granted by Cuba during the U.S. occupation.

11. Cuban dictator Fulgencio Batista seized power in a coup March 10, 1952. He fled the country seven years later, following the victory

of the revolution on January 1, 1959.

12. Rafael Trujillo was dictator of the Dominican Republic from 1930 until his assassination in 1961. Paraguay was ruled by Gen. Alfredo Stroessner from 1954 until his ouster by a military coup in 1989. Nicaragua was ruled by Anastasio Somoza from 1933 until his assassination in 1956. He was then replaced by his son Luis Somoza, who became the new president. Another son, Anastasio Somoza, became head of the National Guard. The latter Somoza assumed the presidency after his brother's death in 1967, and was finally ousted in 1979 by the victory of the Nicaraguan revolution under the leadership of the Sandinista National Liberation Front.

13. On March 31, 1958, the U.S. State Department announced the temporary suspension of a shipment of 1,950 Garand rifles to Batista to allow for "the opportunity of consulting further with the appropriate Cuban officials." The statement was subsequently referred to in the press as an "arms embargo." In May the U.S. State Department authorized the delivery of three hundred aerial rockets to Batista.

14. In adopting the Agrarian Reform Law of May 17, 1959, the new revolutionary government made good on what had been one of the central promises of the July 26 Movement and Rebel Army. A limit of 30 *caballerías* (approximately 1,000 acres) was set on individual landholdings. Implementation of the law resulted in the confiscation of the vast estates and sugar plantations in Cuba—many of them owned by U.S. companies; this land passed into the hands of the new government. The law granted sharecroppers, tenant farmers, and squatters deeds to the land they tilled. A second agrarian reform law, enacted October 4, 1963, set a maximum limit on holdings of 167 acres.

15. In the early 1950s the Guatemalan regime of Jacobo Arbenz carried out a number of democratic measures that earned it the enmity of Washington. The most important of these was an agrarian reform that struck at the vast holdings of the United Fruit Company. The U.S. government orchestrated a ferocious campaign against the "Communist menace" in Guatemala, and the CIA masterminded a coup in 1954 that installed a right-wing dictatorship led by Col. Carlos Castillo Armas.

16. The sugar quota was the amount of Cuban sugar allowed by Washington to be sold in the U.S. market.

17. This analogy comes from the book *The Fable of the Shark and the Sardines: The Strangulation of Latin America*, by Juan José Arévalo, president of Guatemala from 1945 to 1951.

18. The bombing of Cuban sugar mills and cane fields by planes taking off from the United States began in October 1959.

19. The incident Castro is describing took place on October 21, 1959. In the attack two were killed and forty-seven wounded.

20. On March 4, 1960, the French ship *La Coubre*, bringing Belgian munitions, blew up in the Havana harbor, killing eighty-one people.

21. On February 18, 1960, a plane blew up while attempting to bomb a Cuban sugar mill. The body of pilot Robert Ellis Frost, a U.S. citizen, was recovered in the wreckage.

22. On May 1, 1960, a U.S. U-2 spy plane was shot down over the Soviet Union and the pilot captured. The plane was more than 1,200 miles inside Soviet territory.

23. On February 13, 1960, the first Cuban-Soviet trade agreement was signed, in which the USSR agreed to buy one million tons of Cuban sugar a year for the next five years at world market prices.

24. On July 2, 1960, the U.S. House of Representatives approved a bill authorizing the reduction of Cuba's sugar quota. The bill was signed by President Dwight D. Eisenhower the following day. On July 6, Eisenhower ordered a cut in Cuba's sugar quota by 700,000 tons.

25. In the Mexican War of 1846–48 the United States seized Mexican territory extending from the Oklahoma Panhandle to the Pacific Ocean. On September 13, 1846, after U.S. troops took Chapultepec Hill in Mexico City, six Mexican cadets refused to surrender and, with the Mexican flag, jumped from cliffs to their deaths.

26. U.S. troops were sent to Mexico several times during the Mexican revolution that began in 1910. Nicaragua faced direct U.S. military intervention a number of times in the nineteenth century and in 1910, 1912–25, and 1926–33; in 1927 Augusto César Sandino organized an army of peasants and workers that fought a guerrilla war to drive out the U.S. troops, who finally left in 1933. Haiti was attacked by U.S. troops in 1914 and again in 1915; the country was militarily occupied until 1934. The Dominican Republic was attacked by U.S. forces in 1903, 1904, 1912–14, 1916–24, and 1965.

27. The Organization of American States (OAS) held its Seventh Consultative Meeting of Foreign Ministers of the American Republics in San José, Costa Rica, in late August 1960. There the OAS approved the Declaration of San José. This document, an attack on the Cuban revolution, asserted that all member states were "under obligation to submit to the discipline of the Inter-American system." The Cuban delegation

submitted a counterresolution and walked out after it was defeated.

28. Fulfilling a goal raised by Fidel Castro in his 1953 courtroom speech "History Will Absolve Me," which became the program of the Cuban revolutionaries, in 1959 the revolutionary government started turning many of Batista's army garrisons into schools.

29. Castro's statement here was the first public announcement of Cuba's plans for a national literacy drive. From late 1960 through the end of 1961 the revolutionary government organized a successful campaign to teach one million Cubans to read and write. Central to this effort was the mobilization of 100,000 young people to go to the countryside, where they lived with peasants whom they were teaching. As a result of this drive, Cuba virtually eliminated illiteracy.

30. At an inter-American conference in Bogotá, Colombia, September 5–13, 1960, U.S. undersecretary of state Douglas Dillon proposed a "broad new social development program for Latin America, dedicated to supporting the self-help efforts of the governments and peoples of Latin America." Cuba was the only Latin American government that opposed the U.S. plan, putting forward a number of alternative proposals that included the creation of a fund for economic development of $3 billion a year for ten years. For an analysis of the U.S. program for Latin American development launched in 1961 as the Alliance for Progress, see Ernesto Che Guevara's speech to the Geneva Conference on Trade and Development elsewhere in this volume.

31. The Swan Islands (Islas del Cisne) are two islands in the Caribbean off the coast of Honduras. In 1863 they were taken over by the U.S. government. Following the Cuban revolution, the U.S. government used the islands to make counterrevolutionary radio broadcasts to Cuba. In 1971 Washington agreed to recognize Honduran sovereignty over the islands, although the U.S. maintained its radio station.

32. The U.S. naval base at Guantánamo on the southeast coast of Cuba was established during the U.S. occupation at the beginning of the twentieth century. Under the terms of the agreement imposed on Cuba, Washington's tenure over the base had no time limit and could be abrogated or modified only by mutual agreement. Over the protests of the Cuban people and government, the Guantánamo base remains there to this day.

33. At the time Sen. John F. Kennedy was the Democratic Party candidate for president in the November 1960 election. Kennedy's Republican opponent was Vice President Richard Nixon. Kennedy won the elec-

tion and became president in January 1961.

34. The Monroe Doctrine, enunciated by President James Monroe in 1823, outlined the United States government policy of seeking to break the stranglehold of the powerful European monarchies over their colonial empires in the Americas. From the closing decades of the nineteenth century onward, as the United States became an imperialist world power, the Monroe Doctrine was increasingly cited as the justification for U.S. political and military intervention against the nations of Latin America and the Caribbean that were trying to break the stranglehold of U.S. domination.

35. This is a reference to an incident that occurred at the airport shortly after Castro's arrival. At one point the motorcade carrying the Cuban delegation stopped and Castro began waving to a crowd of several thousand supporters there to greet him. A New York City cop then shoved Castro's arm back into the car in rough fashion.

36. The Greek calends is a time that will never arrive. In the calendar of ancient Rome, calends were the first day of the month, from which the remaining days were counted. The ancient Greeks did not use the Roman calendar.

37. Following Egypt's nationalization of the Suez Canal in 1956, the country was invaded by British, French, and Israeli troops.

Indonesia, formerly a Dutch colony, proclaimed its independence in 1945; for several years the new republic faced repeated armed attacks by Dutch and British troops.

38. After the Congo (today Zaire) won its independence from Belgium in June 1960, Washington and its allies moved quickly to destabilize the new government headed by Prime Minister Patrice Lumumba, who had been the leader of the independence struggle. In July 1960, Moise Tshombe began a war against the new regime by declaring the secession of the southern province of Katanga (today Shaba), with himself as president. Lumumba's government appealed to the United Nations for help, and UN troops were sent as a "peacekeeping force." Washington and its allies moved swiftly to disarm Lumumba's forces, sending Belgian and UN troops into the capital, Léopoldville. They also backed the proimperialist breakaway regime set up by Tshombe in Katanga and promoted other dissident movements.

The U.S.-led intervention succeeded by late 1960 in winning over a faction within the Congolese government, headed by army chief of staff Mobutu Sese Seko, and Lumumba was deposed in September. He was later arrested and handed over to Tshombe's forces, who murdered him in January 1961. For an analysis of subsequent events, see Guevara's December 1964 address to the General Assembly elsewhere in this volume.

39. Algeria, then a French colony, was waging a war for its independence. In 1962, after eight years of war, France signed a cease-fire with the liberation forces, agreeing to recognize Algerian independence.

40. At a mass rally in Havana on August 6, 1960, the Cuban government responded to Washington's cut in Cuba's sugar quota by announcing the nationalization of the holdings of the principal U.S. companies in Cuba, including oil refineries, sugar mills, and telephone and electricity utilities.

41. Kwame Nkrumah helped lead the Gold Coast (renamed Ghana) to independence from Britain in 1957 and was prime minister and later president from 1957 to 1966. Sékou Touré was a leader of the struggle for independence in Guinea, which won its independence from France in 1958; he served as president from then until his death in 1984. Gamal Abdel Nasser was prime minister and later president of Egypt from 1954 until his death in 1970. Under his leadership the Egyptian government nationalized the Suez Canal.

42. In his address three days earlier, Soviet premier Khrushchev announced a new proposal on disarmament to the General Assembly, based on an earlier proposal to a June 1960 East-West disarmament conference. He called for a ban on production, stockpiling, and use of nuclear weapons and immediate destruction of all means of delivering them, as well as abolition of foreign military bases.

43. At the time, China's UN seat was occupied by the government of Taiwan. In 1971 the People's Republic of China assumed the seat.

44. The Blue Division was a contingent of 18,000 troops from Spain that was organized in 1941 and sent to fight alongside the invading German army in the Soviet Union. Spain's government at the time was headed by Gen. Francisco Franco, who had come to power following the civil war of 1936–39, with the military support of the German and Italian fascist regimes. Franco remained the head of the Spanish government until his death in 1975.

45. Following World War II, the U.S. Seventh Fleet aided the regime of Chiang Kai-shek in its war against the revolutionary upsurge of China's workers and peasants. After the defeat of the U.S.-backed dictatorship in 1949 and its withdrawal to the island of Taiwan, the U.S. fleet helped

ensure the consolidation of Chiang's regime on Taiwan.

46. The Abraham Lincoln Brigade was made up of volunteers from the United States who fought in the Spanish civil war against the Franco-led forces.

47. Novelist Waldo Frank, a supporter of the revolution, visited Cuba in 1959 and wrote the book *Cuba: Prophetic Island* in 1961. Correspondent Carleton Beals, author of *The Crime of Cuba* and a score of other books on Latin America and the Caribbean, wrote numerous articles in defense of the revolution.

48. The First Declaration of Havana was issued on September 2, 1960, in reply to the Declaration of San José by the Organization of American States, a sharp attack on the Cuban revolution. The document was read aloud by Castro at a rally of close to a million people (referred to as the National General Assembly of the People of Cuba), and approved by acclamation. A Second Declaration of Havana was issued February 4, 1962. (See footnote 63.)

49. The Movement of Nonaligned Countries has its origins in an April 1955 conference of Asian and African governments in Bandung, Indonesia. That meeting, held in the midst of a struggle sweeping Africa and Asia to throw off colonial rule, adopted a ten-point declaration of principles concerning relations between sovereign states. The principles included mutual respect for territorial integrity and sovereignty; nonaggression; noninterference in a country's internal affairs; the equality of nations and races; peaceful coexistence; and economic cooperation. In 1961 the first Nonaligned summit conference was held in Belgrade, Yugoslavia, with twenty-five member countries. Cuba was a founding member.

Holding summit meetings every three years, the Nonaligned Movement has grown to include the majority of the world's underdeveloped countries, most of whom share a history of imperialist domination. As a result, Nonaligned summit meetings over the years have adopted anti-colonialist and anti-imperialist positions on many issues. Nevertheless, because of its politically and economically heterogeneous composition—ranging from governments closely allied to Washington and other imperialist powers all the way to Cuba—the Nonaligned meetings have often been the arena of sharp conflicts.

50. At the instigation of the U.S. government, Cuba was expelled from the Organization of American States (OAS) in January 1962.

51. A UN Conference on Trade and Employment was held in Havana

from November 1947 to March 1948. It adopted the Havana Charter, which was to be the charter of a new international body to be known as the International Trade Organization. This organization never came into being, however, largely as the result of the U.S. government's refusal to become part of it. Instead, many of its anticipated functions were assumed by the General Agreement on Tariffs and Trade (GATT).

52. Bretton Woods, New Hampshire, was the site of a July 1944 conference that led to the creation of two major lending agencies in which the U.S. government played a decisive role: the International Monetary Fund and the International Bank for Reconstruction and Development, popularly known as the World Bank.

53. The General Agreement on Tariffs and Trade (GATT) went into effect in 1948. Like the International Monetary Fund and World Bank, GATT was one of the international entities created at the initiative of the U.S. capitalist class following its victory in the Second World War in order to help maintain its dominant industrial and trading position vis-à-vis its imperialist rivals, and maintain economic domination over the colonial and semicolonial world.

GATT's stated principles are nondiscrimination, reciprocity, and the elimination of quotas. GATT negotiations, however, reflect the shifting relationship of forces between the governments of the various capitalist competitors adhering to it.

54. See note 43.

55. This is a reference to Namibia (South-West Africa), which had been a South African colony since 1920, under the authorization of the League of Nations. In 1946 the United Nations called for South Africa to submit a new trusteeship agreement. This request was rejected by the government of South Africa, which maintained that the UN had no right to challenge its occupation of Namibia. In 1966 the UN General Assembly voted to strip South Africa of its mandate.

South Africa agreed to abide by the UN decision only after the defeat of its forces in a decisive 1988 battle at Cuito Cuanavale in southern Angola at the hands of Cuban, Angolan, and SWAPO (South-West Africa People's Organisation) forces. Namibia became independent in 1990.

56. See note 38.

57. On April 17, 1961, 1,500 Cuban-born mercenaries invaded Cuba at the Bay of Pigs on the southern coast. The action, organized by Washington, aimed to establish a "provisional government" to appeal for direct U.S. intervention. However, the invaders were defeated within

seventy-two hours by the militia and the Revolutionary Armed Forces. On April 19, the last invaders surrendered at Playa Girón (Girón Beach), which is the name Cubans use to designate the battle.

58. This is a reference to the 1962 October crisis. It is known in the United States as the "Cuban missile crisis," the term used by the Kennedy administration and popularized since then by the daily press. The crisis began when President John F. Kennedy ordered a total blockade of Cuba, threatened an invasion of the island, and placed U.S. forces throughout the world on nuclear alert. Washington demanded the removal of Soviet nuclear missiles which had been installed in Cuba by mutual agreement of the two sovereign powers. Cuban workers and farmers responded by mobilizing massively in defense of the revolution. Following an exchange of communications between Moscow and Washington, Soviet premier Nikita Khrushchev decided to remove the missiles—without consulting the Cuban government.

59. The Alliance for Progress was a U.S.-sponsored program established in 1961 as a response to the Cuban revolution and its example. It allocated $20 billion in loans to Latin American governments over a ten-year period in exchange for their compliance in lining up against Cuba. For more on the Alliance for Progress, see "The Real Meaning of the Alliance for Progress (At Punta del Este)" in *Che Guevara and the Cuban Revolution* (New York: Pathfinder, 1987).

60. Enacted in October 1962 by the U.S. Congress, the Trade Expansion Act gave the president authority to lower tariffs up to 50 percent below their 1962 level.

61. Castro addressed the Sixth Plenary Session of the economic council of the Organization of American States—the "Committee of Twenty-one"—meeting in Buenos Aires, Argentina, on May 2, 1959.

Punta del Este, Uruguay, was the site of the August 1961 meeting of the Inter-American Economic and Social Council, sponsored by the OAS, at which Washington presented its plans for the Alliance for Progress.

62. Fidel Castro returned to this theme in a 1985 interview: "Twenty-four years ago, Kennedy promoted the Alliance for Progress as an antidote to prevent social convulsions," Castro stated. "He proposed reforms and economic aid totalling $20 billion over several years. . . .

"In recent years the net drain of capital from Latin America alone reached $55 billion. Now the debt reaches the terrifying figure of $360 billion and the interest due on this will reach $400 billion in ten years. The population is now twice as large as twenty-four years ago and the social problems have multiplied. The foreign debt is eighteen times greater than what Kennedy proposed as aid and the interest payments are $40 billion a year, $400 billion in ten years." Fidel Castro, February 13, 1985, interview with Spanish News Agency, in *War and Crisis in the Americas* (New York: Pathfinder, 1985), p. 184.

63. The Second Declaration of Havana was issued by the revolutionary leadership February 4, 1962. It was read and approved by acclamation at a mass rally of one million in Havana. The document was drawn up in reply to the decision taken by the Organization of American States on January 31 to expel Cuba from the organization. The OAS meeting also called on all governments in the hemisphere to cut economic ties and break diplomatic relations with Cuba. On February 3, Washington ordered an almost total embargo on U.S.-Cuban trade.

The text of the Second Declaration of Havana is available in a pamphlet of the same name published by Pathfinder. Also included is the First Declaration of Havana issued September 1960.

64. The Inter-American Economic and Social Council, a commission of the Organization of American States, sponsored a meeting in February 1964 in Alta Gracia, Argentina. This gathering issued a charter constituting a trade negotiations body called the Special Committee for Latin American Coordination.

65. Guinea won independence from Portugal in 1974; Angola won independence in 1975, as did the former Portuguese colony of Mozambique. Vietnam was reunified in 1975.

66. Cuban president Osvaldo Dorticós attended the Second Summit Conference of Nonaligned Countries held October 1964 in Cairo, Egypt. For background on the Nonaligned Movement see note 49.

67. The 1954 Geneva Accords divided the former French colony of Indochina into North and South Vietnam, Laos, and Cambodia. Although the agreement stipulated that Laos was to be independent and neutral, Washington sought to impose a pro-U.S. regime in that country. By the early 1960s this U.S. effort had led to a civil war between the government and the Laotian liberation forces. In May 1961 the Geneva conference was reconvened and in July 1962 a new agreement was reached based on an end to the fighting and the creation of a coalition government that included forces from both sides in the war. This agreement also rapidly fell apart.

As the U.S. government escalated its attacks on the liberation forces in neighboring Vietnam—particularly after the staged Gulf of Tonkin incident in August 1964—it began bombing some of the mountain paths (the so-called Ho Chi Minh Trail) over which supplies carried from North Vietnam to South Vietnam passed through Laotian and Cambodian territory.

68. Cyprus won independence from Britain in 1960, although it was forced to accept a continued British military presence. To maintain its domination, the British crown had long sought to provoke conflicts between the Greek majority and the Turkish minority on the island. In early 1964, after a series of clashes, London sent in troops despite the objection of the Cypriot government. Plans were then announced by Washington and London for a NATO "peacekeeping" force. In March the United Nations Security Council voted to send a UN contingent, which soon arrived. In August 1964, the Turkish government, a member of NATO, ordered its air force to strafe and bomb Greek Cypriot areas of the island.

In 1974 the Turkish government invaded Cyprus and partitioned the island. In 1983 it established a separate regime under its domination in the north.

69. See note 65.

70. Pedro Albizu Campos, leader of the Puerto Rican Nationalist Party, was imprisoned by the U.S. government for proindependence activities in 1937–43, 1950–53, and 1954–64. He was released shortly before his death in 1965.

The term "Our America" was first used by Cuban national hero José Martí, who viewed the struggle for Cuba's independence as part of the broader struggle against U.S. imperialist domination of Latin America as a whole.

71. In January 1964 U.S. forces opened fire on Panamanian students demonstrating in the U.S.-occupied Canal Zone, sparking several days of street fighting. More than twenty Panamanians were killed and three hundred were wounded.

72. Cheddi Jagan had become prime minister of British Guiana after the People's Progressive Party won the 1953 elections; shortly thereafter the British colonial authorities sent in troops, ousted the elected government, and suspended the constitution. Jagan was elected again in 1957 and reelected in 1961, despite overt and covert attempts by both the British and U.S. governments to bring down the PPP government. In 1964 Jagan was defeated in an election by Forbes Burnham. The British government granted Guyana its independence in 1966.

73. Forced into exile in 1963, Tshombe had returned to power in June 1964 with U.S. backing.

74. In mid-1964, almost four years after the ouster and murder of Prime Minister Patrice Lumumba described in note 38, a new revolt broke out in the Congo led by Lumumba's followers. In an effort to crush the uprising, during November 1964 U.S. planes bombed rebel-held villages and ferried Belgian troops and mercenaries to these areas. Thousands of Congolese were massacred.

75. After returning to Cuba at the conclusion of his three-month trip, Guevara disappeared from public view, resigned his posts in the government, and, with the backing of Cuba's revolutionary leadership, left the country and went to the Congo. There, at the head of a contingent of Cuban volunteers, he spent several months fighting alongside forces loyal to murdered Prime Minister Patrice Lumumba.

76. Zimbabwe (Southern Rhodesia) won its independence in 1980; Namibia (South-West Africa) in 1990; Lesotho (Basutoland) in 1966; Botswana (Bechuanaland) in 1966; Swaziland in 1968; Djibouti (French Somaliland) in 1977; Yemen (Aden and the Protectorates) in 1967. Oman, formally independent, remains a British protectorate ruled by an absolute monarch.

77. In the 1960s a series of economic, diplomatic, and military clashes occurred between the government of Malaysia, a federation of former British colonies formed in 1963, and Indonesia. Indonesian president Sukarno protested the establishment of the federation as a scheme to "save for the imperialists" the region's rich holdings in tin, rubber, and oil.

78. An OAS conference in July 1964 called on all its members to break diplomatic relations and suspend trade with Cuba. The meeting charged Cuba with following a "policy of aggression" for allegedly smuggling arms to Venezuelan guerrillas. The Rio Treaty, invoked as justification for this action, was the Inter-American Treaty of Reciprocal Assistance, signed by twenty-one governments September 2, 1947, in Rio de Janeiro. It declared that aggression against any treaty member state would be considered an attack on all of them.

79. The Taiwan regime was expelled from the UN in 1971 after the People's Republic of China was seated.

80. The Federal Republic of Germany (West Germany) and the German Democratic Republic (East Germany) were both admitted to the United Nations in 1973. Germany was reunified in 1990.

81. The United Nations Conference on Trade and Development at Geneva held March-June 1964 approved a series of ten general principles, most of which were opposed by the U.S. delegation. A number of these principles stood in direct contradiction to Washington's blockade of Cuba. These included a statement that economic relations between countries should be based on the principles of sovereignty, noninterference, and self-determination; that there should be no economic discrimination because of a country's socioeconomic system; and that each country had the right to freely trade with other countries.

82. See note 32.

83. Dominican dictator Rafael Trujillo was assassinated on May 30, 1961. In November 1961, in the context of a growing rebellion by the Dominican people triggered by the return to Santo Domingo of two of Trujillo's brothers, Washington sent warships off the Dominican coast. In April 1965, four months after Guevara's address, over twenty thousand U.S. troops invaded the Dominican Republic to crush a popular uprising.

In April 1948 the assassination of Colombian Liberal Party leader Jorge E. Gaitán sparked a rebellion that became known as the *Bogotazo*.

84. Costa Rica's representative had stated: "I must categorically deny the existence in Costa Rica of training camps for troops of Cuban or of any other nationality. When rumors of the existence of such camps appeared in our press—a free and democratic press and one that is certainly very different from that existing in Cuba—the journalists demanded that there should be a complete investigation. The government complied and the journalists themselves participated constantly in the investigation. The rumors turned out to be completely unfounded."

85. Manuel Artime, known as "the golden boy of the CIA," was the leader of Brigade 2506, the counterrevolutionary exile force organized by the U.S. government, which invaded Cuba at the Bay of Pigs in April 1961.

86. Nicaraguan UN representative Ortega Urbina had denied that any camps had been established in Nicaragua to train Cuban counterrevolutionaries. To attempt to "link my government and my country with alleged future invasion attempts by Cubans against Cuba," Ortega Urbina concluded, "would be like attempting to blame my government for the fact that Cuban international policy today is written in Russian and is spoken in Spanish with an Argentine accent."

87. José Martí is one of Cuba's national heroes. A noted poet and

writer, he founded the Cuban Revolutionary Party in 1892 and launched the country's final independence war in 1895. He was killed in battle in 1895.

88. On April 24, 1959, an expedition of more than eighty armed men, half of them Cubans, landed in Panama. Since the force had sailed from Cuba and was commanded by a Cuban, César Vega, it was claimed that the expedition was sponsored by the revolutionary government. This claim was denied by the Cuban government, which publicly condemned the adventure. A week after the landing, the group surrendered without resistance.

Barbudos, or "bearded ones," was a popular term in Cuba for the Rebel Army fighters in the war against the Batista dictatorship.

89. In 1903, after unsuccessful negotiations with the Colombian government to build a canal across what at the time was Colombia's province of Panama, U.S. marines landed in Colón in support of a "revolt" to establish Panamanian independence. The new government signed a treaty allowing Washington to build and control the canal.

90. In his address to a 1961 conference sponsored by the OAS in Punta del Este, Uruguay, Guevara had read portions of a secret U.S. government report prepared for its ambassador to Venezuela, Teodoro Moscoso, which had come into Cuban hands. The document expressed concern that the corruption and incompetence of Venezuela's rulers had reached a point where they could no longer be reliably counted on to suppress a revolt by workers and peasants. The report argued that the country's ruling millionaire families would have to give up "part of their status quo and wealth" or "be faced with the loss of both (and very possibly their own death at the hands of a firing squad)." See Che Guevara, "The Real Meaning of the Alliance for Progress," in *Che Guevara and the Cuban Revolution*, pp. 291–96.

91. COPEI, the Christian Social Party, is one of Venezuela's two main capitalist parties.

92. The version presented by Washington at the time was that the April 15, 1961, U.S.-organized bombing of Cuba's airports—the prelude to the Bay of Pigs invasion—had been carried out by disenchanted members of Cuba's own air force, who had then flown to the United States to seek "political asylum."

93. *Gusano*, meaning "worm," is a term popularly used in Cuba to refer to counterrevolutionaries.

94. Stevenson had termed Guevara "a man with a long Communist,

revolutionary record in Latin America, only the latter portion of which has been devoted to Cuba."

95. Stevenson had stated: "We do not support or condone hit-and-run attacks against ships in the Cuban trade, or against other targets in Cuba. We are taking, as I have often repeated in these halls, all precautions to ensure that raids are not launched, manned, or equipped from United States territory."

96. Stevenson had claimed that the charge of a U.S. embargo on medicines "is completely without foundation. We are strictly following the decision of the OAS of 26 July 1964, which excepted food stuffs, medicines, and medical supplies, provided for humanitarian purposes, from the economic measures applied to the Castro regime."

97. The Fifth Nonaligned Summit Conference was held in Colombo, Sri Lanka, August 16–19, 1976.

98. The second Strategic Arms Limitation Treaty, known as SALT II, was signed in June 1979 by Soviet president Leonid Brezhnev and U.S. president James Carter. The agreement set ceilings on the number of each country's intercontinental ballistic missiles. The U.S. Senate refused to ratify the treaty.

99. Zimbabwe (formerly the white settler state of Southern Rhodesia) won independence in April 1980. Namibia, the former South African colony known as South-West Africa, became independent in March 1990.

Mozambique, following independence in 1975, faced a lengthy war against Renamo, a reactionary guerrilla army organized and financed by the governments of Southern Rhodesia and South Africa.

Zambia, after attaining independence in 1964, suffered repeated attacks by South African and Rhodesian forces raiding camps and settlements of exiled Namibian and Zimbabwean freedom fighters.

Angola, from the time it won independence in 1975 until 1991, faced a South African-supported guerrilla war waged by UNITA; it was also the target of repeated incursions by the South African army.

Botswana, after attaining independence in 1966, suffered numerous attacks by Rhodesian troops.

Lesotho, independent since 1966 but completely surrounded by South African territory, faced ongoing pressure from Pretoria to expel supporters of the then-outlawed African National Congress who had taken refuge there.

100. The Patriotic Front of Zimbabwe was made up of the two main

organizations fighting for independence against the settler state of Southern Rhodesia—the Zimbabwe African People's Union, headed by Joshua Nkomo; and the Zimbabwe African National Union, headed by Robert Mugabe. SWAPO, the South-West Africa People's Organisation, led the struggle for Namibia's independence.

101. Western Sahara, relinquished as a colony by Spain in 1976, was occupied militarily by the governments of Morocco and Mauritania; Mauritania subsequently withdrew its forces and renounced all claims to the territory. A struggle for that country's independence has been led by the Polisario Front.

102. Mayotte, the most populous of the Comoro Islands in the Indian Ocean, remains a colony of France. Four of the Malagasy Islands— the Glorieuses, Juan de Nova, Europa, and Bassa de India—were separated from Madagascar and retained as French colonies when Madagascar attained independence in 1960.

103. UN General Assembly Resolution 3236, approved November 22, 1974, reaffirmed the right of the Palestinian people to self-determination, national independence, and sovereignty.

104. The text of Castro's keynote address to the Sixth Summit Conference of the Movement of Nonaligned Countries is contained in *Fidel Castro Speeches: Cuba's Internationalist Foreign Policy 1975–80* (New York: Pathfinder, 1981), pp. 162–79.

105. Following Cairo's defeat in the 1973 war with Israel, accords between Egyptian president Anwar al-Sadat and Israeli prime minister Menachem Begin were signed at the U.S. presidential resort at Camp David, Maryland, in September 1978. Under terms of a subsequent peace treaty, signed in Washington in March 1979, Cairo extended formal diplomatic recognition to the Israeli state.

106. The Malvinas Islands, located in the South Atlantic three hundred miles off the coast of Argentina, were seized from Argentina by British forces in the nineteenth century and have since been a colony of Britain, which calls them the Falklands. In 1982 Argentine troops, asserting the country's sovereignty, retook possession of the Malvinas. In response, British troops, backed by U.S. military intelligence and supply efforts, invaded the islands and reestablished British rule.

Belize was a colony of Britain; it became independent in 1981. The government of neighboring Guatemala claims sovereignty over part of Belize and does not recognize the former colony's independence.

107. Under treaties signed in 1977, Washington agreed to transfer

sovereignty over the canal to Panama on January 1, 2000. Transitional steps toward the transfer began in 1979.

108. On September 23, 1868, in the town of Lares, Ramón Emeterio Betances led an armed revolt against Spanish colonial rule over Puerto Rico and proclaimed the island's independence. The uprising was crushed by Spanish troops. Puerto Rico was seized from Spain by Washington in 1898. After Hong Kong is returned to China in 1997 as scheduled, Puerto Rico will be the largest remaining colony in the world.

109. In Grenada a popular revolutionary upheaval March 13, 1979, led to the establishment of a workers' and farmers' government under the leadership of Maurice Bishop. The revolutionary government was overthrown in October 1983 in a coup led by Deputy Prime Minister Bernard Coard, and Bishop was murdered. For an account of the accomplishments of the Grenadian revolution and its overthrow from within, see *Maurice Bishop Speaks: The Grenada Revolution and Its Overthrow, 1979–83* (New York: Pathfinder, 1983).

On July 19, 1979, a massive insurrection by workers and peasants in Nicaragua culminated in the overthrow of the U.S.-backed Somoza dictatorship and the establishment of a workers' and farmers' government led by the Sandinista National Liberation Front (FSLN). Within two years the U.S. government had organized the initial units of a counterrevolutionary army—the *contras,* as they became known—which waged a well-financed war against the workers and peasants of Nicaragua. By 1987 the contras had been militarily defeated. In 1990 the FSLN lost an election to a coalition of opponents of the revolution. For background on the Nicaraguan revolution and its early years, see *Sandinistas Speak* (New York: Pathfinder, 1982).

110. For background on the Guantánamo base, see note 32. For a description of the U.S. embargo against Cuba, see Guevara's speech to the Geneva Trade and Development Conference earlier in this volume.

111. The United Nations had designated the 1960s as the first Development Decade, and the 1970s as the second. One of the main objectives outlined as a goal for the Second Development Decade was the attainment of a 6 percent average annual rate of growth in the gross national products of the developing countries.

112. The call for a new international economic order was popularized by many of the underdeveloped nations during May 1974 at a special session of the UN General Assembly. The special session discussed demands of the underdeveloped countries for higher prices on raw materi-

als and for accelerated economic development.

The Fifth Session of the United Nations Conference on Trade and Development (UNCTAD) was held in Manila May-June 1979.

113. A round of trade negotiations sponsored by the General Agreement on Tariffs and Trade (GATT) was concluded in April 1979 with the signing of a new agreement in Geneva. The majority of underdeveloped countries boycotted the signing to protest the refusal of the industrially advanced capitalist countries to meet their demands. For background on GATT, see note 51.

114. The Generalized System of Preferences, negotiated in the late 1960s under the auspices of the General Agreement on Tariffs and Trade (GATT), was a minor tariff adjustment in which industrially advanced capitalist countries agreed to grant duty-free admission to a selection of goods from some underdeveloped countries.

115. The Group of 77 is a caucus of United Nations members. Founded in 1964 by seventy-seven governments attending the United Nations Conference on Trade and Development in Geneva, the group represents the industrially underdeveloped countries. Its purpose is to formulate tactics and demands prior to UN-sponsored conferences on economic development. The Group of 77 has since grown to more than 120 members. Over 170 now belong to the United Nations.

116. The Integrated Program for Commodities and the Common Fund were among resolutions adopted by the Fourth Session of UNCTAD in 1976. Their stated aim was to stabilize selected world market prices through voluntary agreements between the governments of the industrially advanced capitalist countries and the underdeveloped countries.

117. The Eighth Session of the Third United Nations Conference on the Law of the Sea was held March-April 1979. Attended by delegations from 159 countries, the meeting sought to formulate a treaty on the international use of the oceans. The session concluded with no general agreement, as the representatives from the United States and other industrially advanced capitalist countries lined up to oppose the regulation of deep-sea mining.

118. The New York City police had given its backing to the formation of the Welcoming Committee. The Harlem precinct was represented at the founding meeting on September 16.

Index

Also from Pathfinder

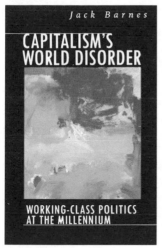

Malcolm X Talks to Young People

"I for one will join in with anyone, I don't care what color you are, as long as you want to change this miserable condition that exists on this earth"—Malcolm X, December 1964. Also includes his 1965 interview with the *Young Socialist* magazine. $10.95

Socialism on Trial

JAMES P. CANNON

The basic ideas of socialism, explained in testimony during the trial of 18 leaders of the Minneapolis Teamsters union and the Socialist Workers Party framed up and imprisoned under the notorious Smith "Gag" Act during World War II. $15.95. Also available in Spanish.

Puerto Rico: Independence Is a Necessity

RAFAEL CANCEL MIRANDA

In two interviews, Puerto Rican independence leader Cancel Miranda—one of five Puerto Rican Nationalists imprisoned by Washington for more than 25 years until 1979—speaks out on the brutal reality of U.S. colonial domination, the campaign to free Puerto Rican political prisoners, the example of Cuba's socialist revolution, and the resurgence of the independence movement today. Also available in Spanish. $3.00

The Revolution Betrayed

What Is the Soviet Union and Where Is It Going?

LEON TROTSKY

In 1917 the working class and peasantry of Russia were the motor force for one of the most profound revolutions in history. Yet within ten years a political counterrevolution by a privileged social layer whose chief spokesperson was Joseph Stalin was being consolidated. This classic study of the Soviet workers state and its degeneration illuminates the roots of the social and political crisis shaking the former Soviet Union today. Also available in Spanish and Russian. $19.95

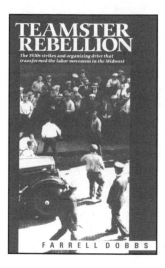

Teamster Rebellion

FARRELL DOBBS

The 1934 strikes that built the industrial union movement in Minneapolis and helped pave the way for the CIO, recounted by a central leader of that battle. The first in a four-volume series on the class-struggle leadership of the strikes and organizing drives that transformed the Teamsters union in much of the Midwest into a fighting social movement and pointed the road toward independent labor political action. $16.95

Socialism: Utopian and Scientific

FREDERICK ENGELS

Modern socialism is not a doctrine, Engels explains, but a working-class movement growing out of the establishment of large-scale capitalist industry and its social consequences. $4.00

To See the Dawn

Baku, 1920—First Congress of the Peoples of the East

How can peasants and workers in the colonial world achieve freedom from imperialist exploitation? By what means can working people overcome divisions incited by their national ruling classes and act together for their common class interests? These questions were addressed by 2,000 delegates to the 1920 Congress of the Peoples of the East. $19.95

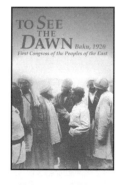

Black Music, White Business

Illuminating the History and Political Economy of Jazz

FRANK KOFSKY

Probes the economic and social conflicts between the artistry of Black musicians and the control by largely white-owned business of jazz distribution— the recording companies, booking agencies, festivals, clubs, and magazines. $15.95

From Pathfinder

The Cuban revolution

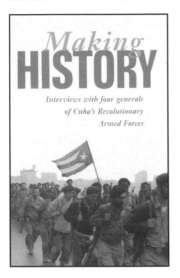

Making History

Interviews with Four Generals of Cuba's Revolutionary Armed Forces
Through the stories of these four outstanding Cuban generals, each with close to half a century of revolutionary activity, we can see the class dynamics that have shaped our entire epoch. We can understand how the people of Cuba, as they struggle to build a new society, have for more than forty years held Washington at bay. With an introduction by Mary-Alice Waters; preface by Juan Almeida. $15.95

Dynamics of the Cuban Revolution

A Marxist Appreciation
Joseph Hansen
How did the Cuban revolution come about? Why does it represent, as Hansen puts it, an "unbearable challenge" to U.S. imperialism? What political challenges has it confronted? Written as the revolution advanced from its earliest days. $20.95

In Defense of Socialism

Fidel Castro

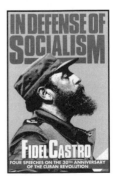

Four Speeches on the 30th Anniversary of the Cuban Revolution, 1988–89
Economic and social progress is possible without the dog-eat-dog competition of capitalism, Castro argues, and socialism remains the only way forward for humanity. Also discusses Cuba's role in the struggle against the apartheid regime in southern Africa. $13.95

in today's world

Che Guevara Talks to Young People

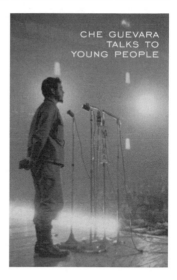

The legendary Argentine-born revolutionary challenges youth of Cuba and the world to work and become disciplined. To fearlessly join the front lines of struggles, small and large. To read and to study. To aspire to be revolutionary combatants. To politicize the organizations they are part of and in the process politicize themselves. To become a different kind of human being as they strive together with working people of all lands to transform the world. And, along this line of march, to renew and revel in the spontaneity and joy of being young. $14.95

Episodes of the Cuban Revolutionary War, 1956–58

Ernesto Che Guevara

A firsthand account of the military campaigns and political events that culminated in the January 1959 popular insurrection that overthrew the Batista dictatorship. With clarity and humor, Guevara describes his own political education. He explains how the struggle transformed the men and women of the Rebel Army and July 26 Movement led by Fidel Castro. Also available in a Spanish edition by Editora Politica. $23.95

Celebrating the Homecoming of Ernesto Che Guevara's Reinforcement Brigade to Cuba

Articles from the *Militant* newspaper on the 30th anniversary of the combat waged in Bolivia by Che and his comrades. $8.00

U.S. Imperialism Has Lost the Cold War . . .

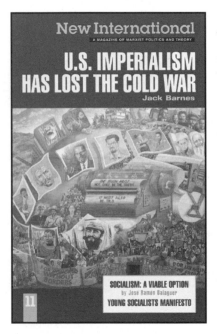

. . . That's what the Socialist Workers Party concluded a decade ago, in the wake of the collapse of regimes and parties across Eastern Europe and in the USSR that claimed to be Communist. Contrary to imperialism's hopes, the working class in those countries had not been crushed. It remains an intractable obstacle to reimposing and stabilizing capitalist relations, one that will have to be confronted by the exploiters in class battles—in a hot war.

Three issues of the Marxist magazine *New International* analyze the propertied rulers' failed expectations and chart a course for revolutionaries in response to the renewed rise of worker and farmer resistance to the economic and social instability, spreading wars, and rightist currents bred by the world market system. They explain why the historic odds in favor of the working class have increased, not diminished, at the opening of the 21st century.

New International no. 11

U.S. Imperialism Has Lost the Cold War *by Jack Barnes* ◆ Socialism: A Viable Option *by José Ramón Balaguer* ◆ Young Socialists Manifesto $14.00

New International no. 10

Imperialism's March toward Fascism and War *by Jack Barnes* ◆ What the 1987 Stock Market Crash Foretold ◆ Defending Cuba, Defending Cuba's Socialist Revolution *by Mary-Alice Waters* ◆ The Curve of Capitalist Development *by Leon Trotsky* $14.00

New International no. 7

Opening Guns of World War III: Washington's Assault on Iraq *by Jack Barnes* ◆ 1945: When U.S. Troops Said "No!" *by Mary-Alice Waters* ◆ Lessons from the Iran-Iraq War *by Samad Sharif* $12.00

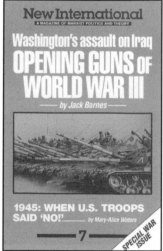

Distributed by Pathfinder

These issues of **New International** are also available in the Spanish **Nueva Internacional**, the French **Nouvelle Internationale**, and the Swedish **Ny International**.

Revolution in Central America and the Caribbean

The Second Assassination of Maurice Bishop

by Steve Clark

The lead article in *New International* no. 6 reviews the accomplishments of the 1979–83 revolution in the Caribbean island of Grenada. Explains the roots of the 1983 coup that led to the murder of revolutionary leader Maurice Bishop, and to the destruction of the workers and farmers government by a Stalinist political faction within the governing New Jewel Movement.

Also in *New International* no. 6:
Washington's Domestic Contra Operation *by Larry Seigle* ◆ Renewal or Death: Cuba's Rectification Process *two speeches by Fidel Castro* ◆ Land, Labor, and the Canadian Revolution *by Michel Dugré*
$15.00

Che Guevara, Cuba, and the Road to Socialism

Articles by Ernesto Che Guevara, Carlos Rafael Rodríguez, Carlos Tablada, Mary-Alice Waters, Steve Clark, Jack Barnes

Exchanges from the early 1960s and today on the political perspectives defended by Guevara as he helped lead working people to advance the transformation of economic and social relations in Cuba. In *New International* no. 8.
$10.00

Distributed by Pathfinder